Author: Rachel Lynette
Editor: Marilyn Evans
Copy Editing: Carrie Gwynne
Art Direction: Cheryl Puckett
Cover Illustration: Nathan Jarvis
Illustration: Jo Larsen
Design/Production: Yuki Meyer

EMC 3391

Evan-Moor®
Helping Children Learn

Visit
teaching-standards.com
to view a correlation
of this book.
This is a free service.

**Correlated to State and
Common Core State Standards**

For information about other Evan-Moor products, call 1-800-777-4362,
fax 1-800-777-4332, or visit our Web site, www.evan-moor.com.
Entire contents © 2009 EVAN-MOOR CORP.
18 Lower Ragsdale Drive, Monterey, CA 93940-5746. Printed in USA.

CPSIA: Bang Printing, 28210 N. Avenue Stanford, Valencia, CA 91355 [11/2015]

CONTENTS

What's in This Book?

Critical and Creative Thinking Activities, Grade 1 contains 46 themes, each presented in a three-page unit that gives students valuable practice with a broad range of thinking skills. The engaging themes will keep students interested and will have them begging to do the next set of activities!

The first and second pages of each unit get students thinking about the topic in a variety of ways. They may be asked to draw on prior knowledge or to generate new ideas.

The last page of each unit features one of a number of stimulating and entertaining formats, including logic puzzles, riddles, and secret codes.

How to Use This Book

• Use the activity pages during your language arts period to keep the rest of the class actively and productively engaged while you work with small groups of students.

• The themed sets of activity pages provide a perfect language arts supplement for your thematic or seasonal units. And you'll find any number of topics that complement your science and social studies curricula.

• Your students will enjoy doing these fun pages for homework or as free-time activities in class.

About the Correlations for This Book

The valuable thinking skills practiced in this book (see inside front cover) are not generally addressed in state standards. However, thinking skills require content to be practiced. The activities in this book have been correlated to the Language Arts and Mathematics standards.

Visit www.teaching-standards.com to view a correlation of this book to your state's standards.

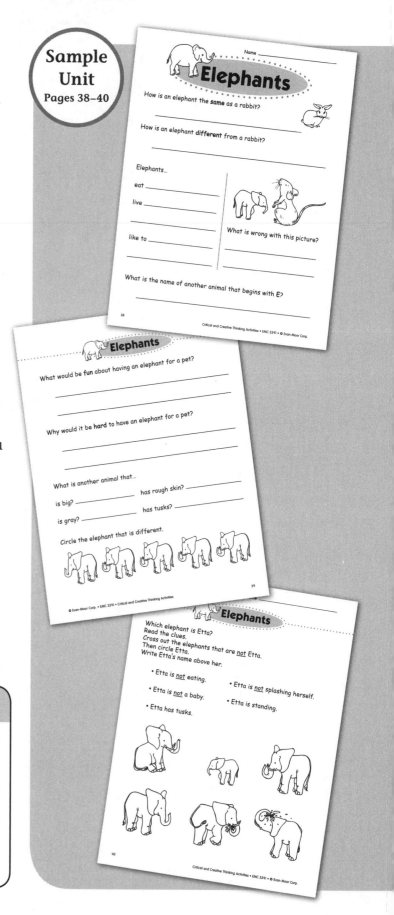

Sample Unit Pages 38–40

Autumn

Color the leaves to make a pattern.
Use **yellow** and **orange**.

In autumn...

the weather _____.

the leaves _____.

people _____.

What will happen next?

_____

_____

_____

Autumn

What sound does it make?

A leaf when you step on it: _____

Rain on the roof: _____

Wind in the trees: _____

1. Draw a tree in autumn.

2. Draw 12 leaves on the tree.

3. Draw 8 leaves on the ground.

4. Draw 3 leaves falling from the tree.

Autumn

The second picture is different from the first picture in 8 ways. Can you find and circle them all?

In autumn, you might have to wear an extra _____.

Winter

What is something you see <u>a lot</u> in winter?

_____

What is something you <u>never</u> see in winter?

_____

Draw the other mitten.

What are 3 different things that you can make from snow?

1. _____

2. _____

3. _____

Number the snowmen from the smallest to the largest.

____   ____   ____   ____   ____

Winter

If you did <u>not</u> have a carrot, what would make a good **nose** for a snowman?

_____

What would make a good **mouth** for a snowman?

_____

What will happen next?

_____

_____

Circle the one that does <u>not</u> belong.

Finish the pattern.

Winter

Which snowman is Sam?
Read the clues and cross out each snowman that is <u>not</u> Sam.
Circle Sam.

- Sam is happy.

- Sam is <u>not</u> wearing a scarf.

- Sam is wearing a hat.

- Sam has a carrot nose.

Name _____

Spring

Number the words
in order from 1 to 5.

_____ water

_____ pick

_____ eat

_____ grow

_____ plant

Draw a flower using <u>only</u> straight lines.

What can you see in spring? _____

What can you hear in spring? _____

What can you feel in spring? _____

What can you smell in spring? _____

✿ Spring

Where does it live?

bird _____

bee _____

frog _____

rabbit _____

Which does <u>not</u> belong? Circle it.

Circle the 4 best **spring** words.

grow	green	garden
rain	babies	warm
blossom	baseball	flowers

Draw the next flower.

✿ Spring

Find the flower pairs.
Color each pair the same way.

Summer

What do you like to do?
Number the activities from 1 to 6.
The one you like the <u>most</u> should be number 1.

_____ hiking   _____ riding a bike

_____ swimming   _____ having a picnic

_____ climbing trees   _____ going to the zoo

Write the opposite.

sunny   _____

hot   _____

wet   _____

play   _____

You made lemonade.
How many glasses do you think you can fill?

_____ glasses of lemonade

Summer

Write something that is true about summer.

_____

Write something that is <u>not</u> true about summer.

_____

Circle the 2 beach balls that are the same size.

Cody forgot to wear sunblock.
How can he keep from getting a sunburn?

_____

_____

_____

Summer

You are going camping.
Draw or write what you will need.

What will you wear?	What will you eat?
Where will you sleep?	What else will you need?

Name _____

Halloween

What are 3 things that scare you?

1. _____

2. _____

3. _____

What scares other people but does <u>not</u> scare you?

_____

Jenna grew 6 big pumpkins and 3 small pumpkins in her garden. How many pumpkins did Jenna grow altogether?

_____ pumpkins

Draw the jack-o'-lantern upside down.

Halloween

Circle the things that you might do at a Halloween party.
Cross off the things that you would <u>not</u> do at a Halloween party.

bob for apples   eat candy   wear a costume

hunt for eggs   open presents   carve a pumpkin

Circle the one that does <u>not</u> belong. Tell someone why.

Finish the pattern.

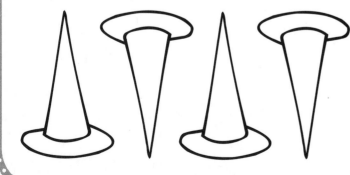

Critical and Creative Thinking Activities • EMC 3391 • © Evan-Moor Corp.

Halloween

Follow the directions to make a Halloween picture.

1. Draw a ghost in the middle window.

2. Draw a different jack-o'-lantern in each corner window.

3. Draw a black cat in the window below the ghost.

4. Draw a spider web in the window above the ghost.

5. Draw something spooky in the last 2 windows.

What are your 3 favorite Thanksgiving foods?

1. _____

2. _____

3. _____

6 people want pumpkin pie.
5 people want apple pie.
How many people want pie?

_____ people want pie.

Would you have wanted to be a Pilgrim? _____

Why or why not? _____

_____

_____

Number the turkeys from the smallest to the largest.

_____   _____   _____   _____   _____

Name _____

Thanksgiving

What are you thankful for?

at home

_____

at school

_____

in nature

_____

Draw 1 thing that you are thankful for.

Circle **Yes** if it is **true**.
Circle **No** if it is **not true**.

Thanksgiving is in November.	Yes	No
Turkey is a vegetable.	Yes	No
Pilgrims came to America.	Yes	No
Indians helped the Pilgrims.	Yes	No
Cranberries are blue.	Yes	No

Circle the one that does <u>not</u> belong.

Thanksgiving

Color each turkey differently.
Use only brown, red, yellow, and orange.

How many times did you use **brown**? _____

How many times did you use **red**? _____

How many times did you use **yellow**? _____

How many times did you use **orange**? _____

 Critical and Creative Thinking Activities • EMC 3391 • © Evan-Moor Corp.

Christmas

On Christmas, what do you...

see? _____

hear? _____

feel? _____

smell? _____

taste? _____

• • • • • • • • • • • • • • • • •

Color each pair of bells differently.

Name _____

Christmas

Which do you like?
Number them from 1 to 6.
The one you like the <u>most</u>
should be number 1.

_____ singing Christmas carols

_____ decorating the tree

_____ making Christmas cookies

_____ opening presents

_____ eating Christmas dinner

_____ seeing Santa Claus

Circle things that can go on
a Christmas tree.

Finish the pattern.

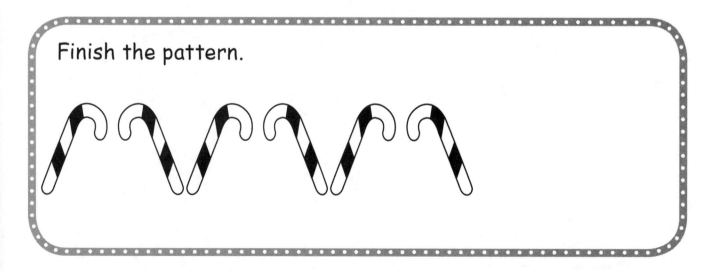

Critical and Creative Thinking Activities • EMC 3391 • © Evan-Moor Corp.

Christmas

Follow the directions to decorate the tree.

1. Color the big round ornaments red.

2. Color the small round ornaments blue.

3. Color the ornaments with a point yellow.

4. Color the lights. Make a pattern.

5. Draw a star on top of the tree.

6. Draw presents under the tree.

7. Color the rest of the tree green.

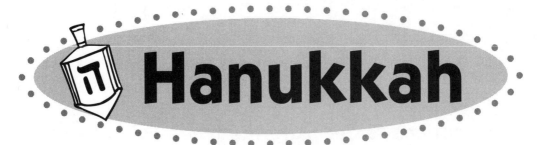

Hanukkah

How many days is Hanukkah? _____

Draw 9 candles on the menorah.
Use yellow and blue.
Make a pattern.

Draw each Hebrew letter on
one of the dreidels.

Number the dreidels in order from the smallest to the largest.

_____   _____   _____   _____   _____

Hanukkah

Make 8 in 8 different ways.

①   5   + ⬡ = 8

②   2   + ⬡ = 8

③ ⬡ +   1   = 8

④ ⬡ +   4   = 8

⑤   9   – ⬡ = 8

⑥ 12   – ⬡ = 8

⑦ ⬡ –   2   = 8

⑧ ⬡ –   4   = 8

This is a Star of David.
How many triangles can you count? _____

How many triangles now? _____

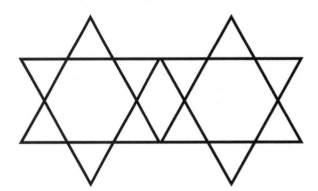

Draw 3 Stars of David.
Make each one a different size.
Color them yellow and blue.

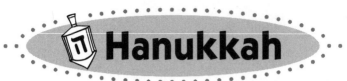 Hanukkah

Rachel gets chocolate coins as a gift on Hanukkah.
She gets 1 coin on the first day, 2 coins on the second day, and so on.
Fill in the chart to see how many coins Rachel gets.

1st Day	✡	1
2nd Day	✡ ✡	2
3rd Day		
4th Day		
5th Day		
6th Day		
7th Day		
8th Day		

How many coins are there in all 8 days?
Write an addition problem to show how many.

____ + ____ + ____ + ____ + ____ + ____ + ____ = ____

 Critical and Creative Thinking Activities • EMC 3391 • © Evan-Moor Corp.

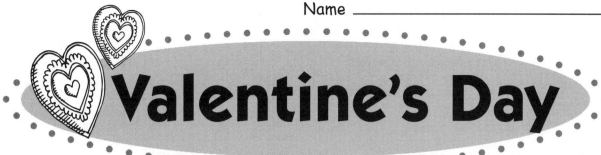

Valentine's Day

Finish each sentence differently.

I love _____.

I love _____.

I love _____.

3 hearts are the same size.
Color them.

What is something that is usually **pink**? _____

What is something that is always **red**? _____

What is something that is always **white**? _____

Valentine's Day

Write a sentence using the words **heart** and **pink**.

_____

_____

How many hearts? _____

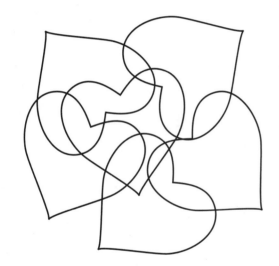

Dani put pink frosting on
6 Valentine's Day cookies.
She put white frosting on
8 cookies.
How many cookies did Dani
frost altogether?

_____ frosted cookies

Finish the patterns.

Valentine's Day

Jordon's valentine cards are missing some letters.
Fill in the letters to show who gets each valentine.

Hanna   **Jacob**   **Maria**   **David**

To: __ a __ __ a

From: Jordon

To: __ a __ __ b

From: Jordon

To: __ __ n n __

From: Jordon

To: __ a __ __ d

From: Jordon

100th
Day of School

I wish I had 100 _____.

Circle the two **100s** that are the same.

100 100 **100** 100 100 100 100

100 100 **100** **100** **100** 100 **100**

Fill in the missing numbers.

10, 20, 30, _____, 50, _____, 70, _____, _____, 100

90, 91, _____, 93, _____, 95, _____, 97, _____, _____, 100

80, 82, 84, 86, _____, 90, _____, _____, 96, _____, 100

If I had $100.00, I would...

_____.

   Critical and Creative Thinking Activities • EMC 3391 • © Evan-Moor Corp.

100th Day of School

What is something that...

costs more than $100.00? _____

weighs more than 100 pounds? _____

goes faster than 100 miles per hour? _____

Are there more than 100 of these in your classroom? Write **yes** or **no**.

crayons _____

books _____

pencils _____

Make the **100** into a face.

100

Divide the dots into groups of 10 dots each.

100th Day of School

Here are 100 circles.
Color the **consonants** yellow.
Color the **vowels** red.

T W Y D V Z

K I B U O E C A I E X

A J A Z N A O B U

C E L I H R J K S N

F O N A Z U I X A

U C E L C T O O L M E R

M H O Q I E R T K I

E V A D B P A Q U X O D

I U M I P J A W

A X S I E F O A I V

P W

What do you see? _____

Cats and Dogs

Which do you like better, **cats** or **dogs**? _____

Why? _____

• • • • • • • • • • • • • • • • •

Write 3 words that describe **cats**.

1. _____

2. _____

3. _____

Which does <u>not</u> belong?

Write 3 <u>different</u> words that describe **dogs**.

1. _____

2. _____

3. _____

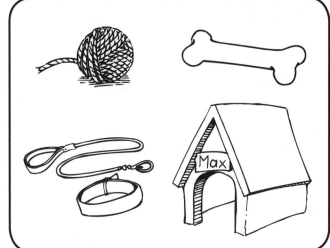

Cats and Dogs

Write **A** for **always** true.
Write **S** for **sometimes** true.
Write **N** for **never** true.

_____ Dogs like bones.   _____ Cats like dogs.

_____ Cats play baseball.   _____ Dogs have paws.

_____ Cats chase mice.   _____ Dogs drive cars.

_____ Dogs chase balls.   _____ Cats are black.

1. Draw a cat and a dog.

2. Make the dog bigger
than the cat.

3. Make the cat yellow.

4. Draw spots on the dog.

Name _____

Cats and Dogs

Read each numbered item below.
Write the number where it belongs in the Venn diagram.
Then make up one of your own.
Write the number in the diagram.

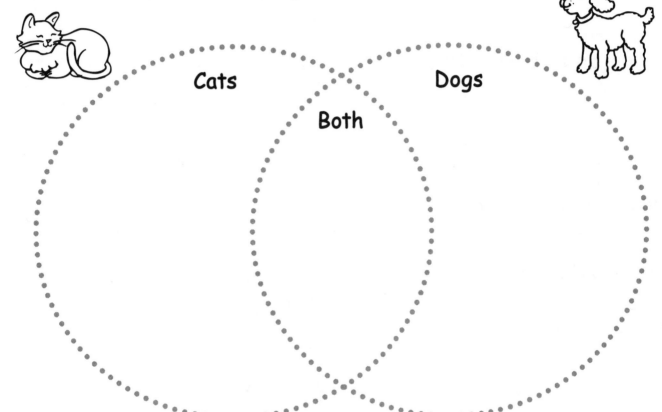

Cats   Dogs

Both

1. barks

2. has whiskers

3. purrs

4. has a tail

5. has sharp teeth

6. likes to fetch

7. feels soft

8. climbs trees

9. can be trained to sit

10. _____

Name _____

Elephants

How is an elephant the **same** as a rabbit?

_____

How is an elephant **different** from a rabbit?

_____

Elephants...

eat _____ .

live _____

_____ .

like to _____

_____ .

What is wrong with this picture?

_____

_____

What is the name of another animal that begins with **E**?

_____

Elephants

What would be **fun** about having an elephant for a pet?

_____

_____

Why would it be **hard** to have an elephant for a pet?

_____

_____

What is another animal that...

is big? _____   has rough skin? _____

is gray? _____   has tusks? _____

Circle the elephant that is different.

Elephants

Which elephant is Etta?
Read the clues.
Cross out the elephants that are <u>not</u> Etta.
Then circle Etta.
Write Etta's name above her.

- Etta is <u>not</u> eating.
- Etta is <u>not</u> a baby.
- Etta has tusks.

- Etta is <u>not</u> splashing herself.
- Etta is standing.

Lions

Write a sentence that is true about lions.

_____

Write a sentence that is <u>not</u> true about lions.

_____

What is another animal that...

hunts for meat? _____

lives in Africa? _____

has babies called **cubs**? _____

Which lion is different?

Write a sentence about lions using the words **cubs** and **hunt**.

_____

 Lions

Why do you think the lion is called "the King of Beasts"?

_____

What other animal would make a good king? _____

Why? _____

Circle the 3 best **lion** words.

strong   brave   furry   hunter   fast   scary

cute   brown   wild   big   quiet   smart

Write the opposite.

fast   _____

wild   _____

sharp   _____

king   _____

What is the name of another animal that begins with L?

_____

Lions

Read each numbered item below.
Does it tell about **lions**, **house cats**, or **both**?
Write the number where it belongs in the Venn diagram.
Then make up one of your own. Write the number in the diagram.

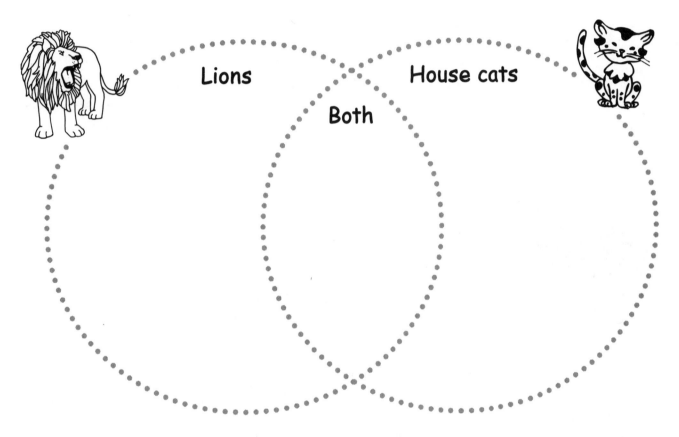

Lions

House cats

Both

1. roars

2. lives in the wild

3. has sharp teeth

4. has a tail

5. uses a litter box

6. has a mane

7. meows

8. can climb trees

9. chases mice

10. _____

Name _____

Giraffes

What could you do if you had a long neck like a giraffe?

_____

What is wrong with this picture?

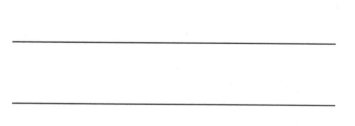

_____

_____

_____

Add spots.

What is the name of another animal that begins with **G**?

_____

Giraffes

Write a sentence that is true about giraffes.

_____

Write a sentence that is <u>not</u> true about giraffes.

_____

Why do giraffes have to spread their legs to drink?

_____

_____

_____

_____

Circle the giraffe parts.

neck	tongue	fins	hooves
trunk	tail	horns	claws

Giraffes

Look at the animals in each row.
Then write why they belong together.

_____

_____

_____

46

Kangaroos

Kangaroos hop.
What are 2 other animals that hop?

_____ and _____

Kangaroos eat grass.
What are 2 other animals that eat grass?

_____ and _____

How many joeys? _____

How many kangaroos? _____

How many ears? _____

A baby kangaroo is called a **joey**.
Add a joey in the pouch.

Kangaroos

A kangaroo's pouch is like a pocket.
If you had a pocket like a kangaroo, what would you put in it?

_____

Write **T** for **true**.
Write **N** for **not true**.

| What other things have pockets?

_____ Kangaroos have fur.

_____ All kangaroos have
pouches.

_____ Kangaroos eat meat.

_____ Kangaroos have
strong tails.

What other things have
pockets?

_____

_____

_____

_____

_____

Number the kangaroos from the smallest to the largest.

____   ____   ____   ____   ____

 Kangaroos

Help Mama Kangaroo cross the river to get to her joey.
She can hop <u>only</u> on stones with **even numbers**.
Color her path.

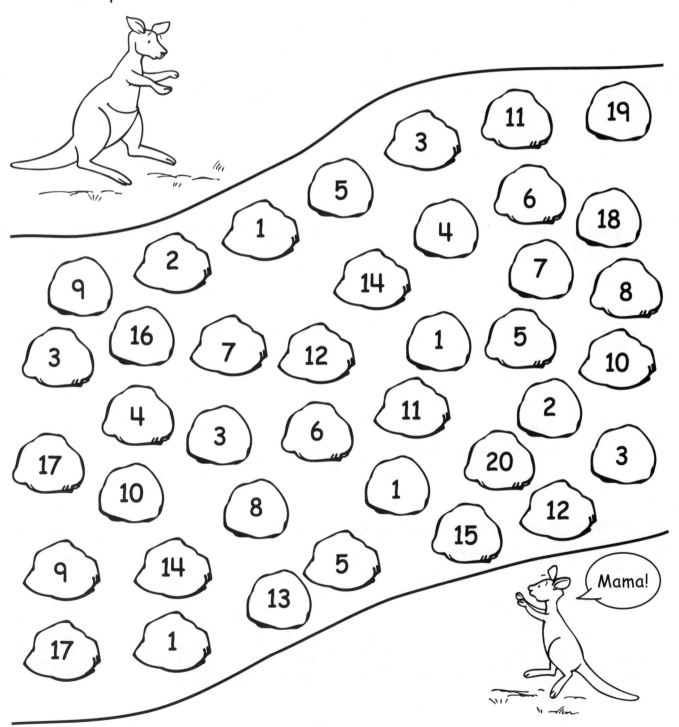

How is a real bear the **same** as a teddy bear?

_____

How is a real bear **different** from a teddy bear?

_____

Can you think of 3 different kinds of bears?	Write 3 words that rhyme with **bear**.
1. _____	1. _____
2. _____	2. _____
3. _____	3. _____

Color the bears. Make a pattern.
Use <u>only</u> **black** and **brown**.

Name _____

 **Bears**

What do bears eat?
Draw or write as many things as you can.

Mama Bear ate **6** fish.
Her 2 cubs ate **3** fish each.
How many fish did the bears
eat altogether?

_____ fish

Which of these prints was
made by a bear? Circle it.

Finish each sentence.

Bears like _____.

Bears need _____.

Bears have _____.

Bears

What is wrong with this picture?
Try to find at least 10 things.
Color them.

Critical and Creative Thinking Activities • EMC 3391 • © Evan-Moor Corp.

Name _____

Snakes

How does a snake...

look? _____

sound? _____

feel? _____

Write words that rhyme with **snake**.

_____

_____

_____

_____

Write **T** for **true**.
Write **N** for **not true**.

_____ Snakes are reptiles.

_____ Snakes have little legs.

_____ Snakes have scales.

_____ Snakes can fly.

Make an **X** on the one that does <u>not</u> belong.

Snakes

Would you like to have a snake for a pet?_____

Why or why not?_____

_____

Color the snake's stripes.
Use this pattern: **ABABC**.

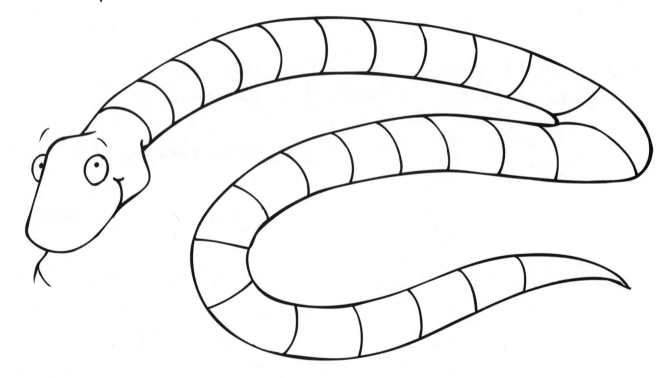

Write the opposite.

long _____   skinny _____

cold _____   dangerous _____

Name _____

Snakes

These 4 snakes are all tangled up.
Color each snake a different color.

Make the word **SNAKE** with snakes!
Draw snakes to make the missing letters.

 **S   A K**

Butterflies

Draw what happens next.

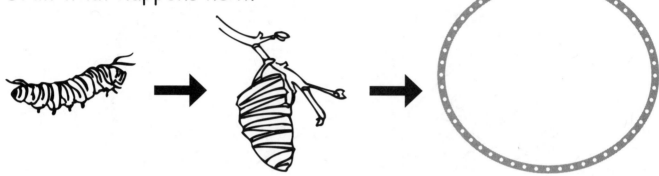

Write 3 words that describe **caterpillars**.

1. _____

2. _____

3. _____

Write 3 words that describe **butterflies**.

1. _____

2. _____

3. _____

These are flutterflies.

These are **not** flutterflies.

Circle the flutterfly.

Butterflies

How is a butterfly the **same** as a bird?

_____

How is a butterfly **different** from a bird?

_____

· ·

1. Draw a caterpillar on the longest leaf.

2. Draw a butterfly on the tallest flower.

3. Draw a flying butterfly.

4. Color the picture.

Butterflies

Make each butterfly's wings match.
Color the pictures.

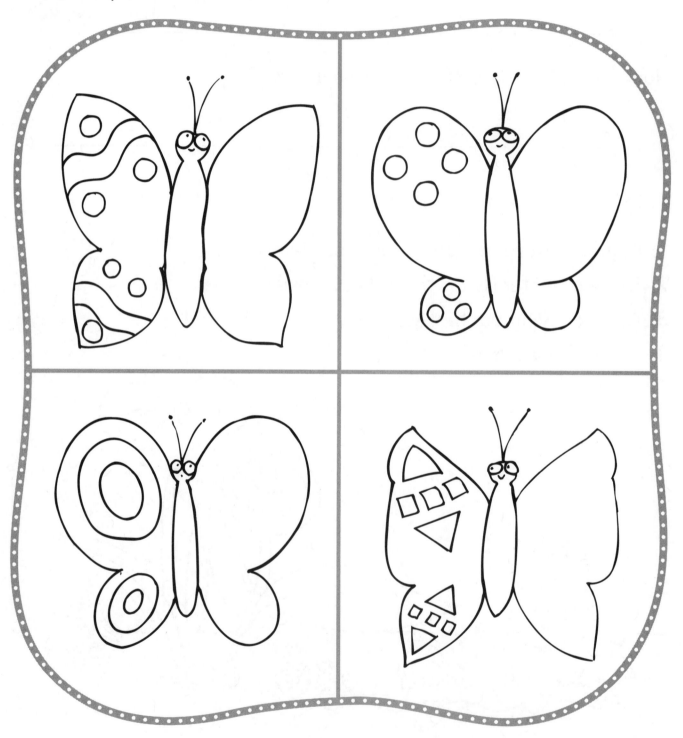

Critical and Creative Thinking Activities • EMC 3391 • © Evan-Moor Corp.

 Ants

Would you find ants in these places?
Write **P** for **probably**.
Write **M** for **maybe**.
Write **N** for **no**.

_____ at a picnic

_____ in your shoe

_____ at the North Pole

_____ in a garden

_____ in the freezer

_____ in the forest

_____ in your desk

_____ on the kitchen table

How many altogether?
Fill in the numbers.

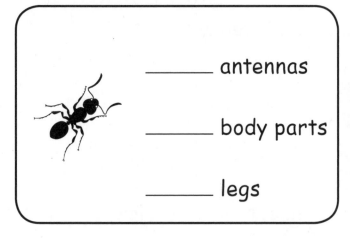

_____ antennas

_____ body parts

_____ legs

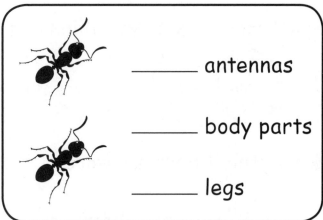

_____ antennas

_____ body parts

_____ legs

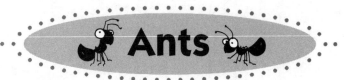

Ants

You find an ant on your **sandwich**. What do you do?

_____

You find an ant in your **juice**. What do you do?

_____

Which ant is different?

Put a O around the first ant.
Draw a □ around the last ant.
Make an X on the middle ant.

How many ants do you think could fit on a penny?

 _____ ants

Circle the 4 best **ant** words.

small	cute	insect	icky
busy	strong	quick	brave

Help Alvin Ant collect as many crumbs as he can
on his way back to the anthill.
Draw a path.
Try to get at least 15 crumbs.

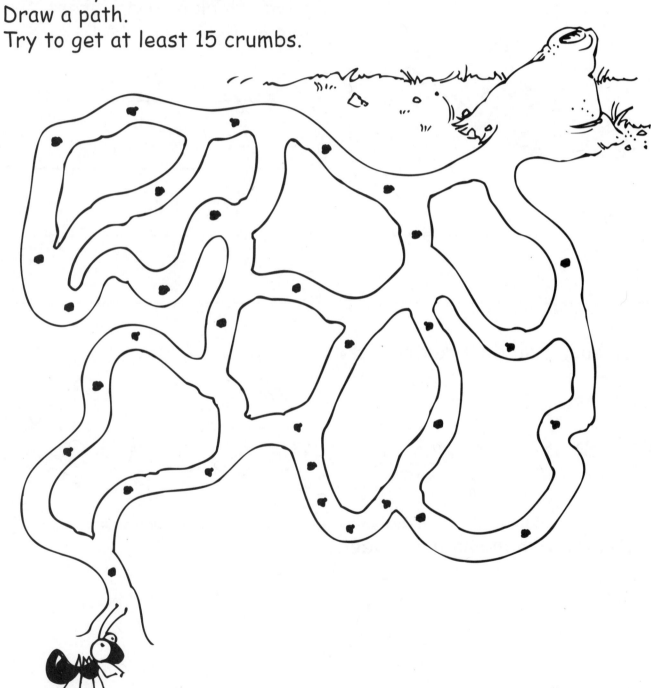

How many crumbs did Alvin get? _____

Fish

What happens next?

_____

_____

Can you think of 4 different kinds of fish?

1. _____

2. _____

3. _____

4. _____

Color each fish differently.

Draw a fish hiding in seaweed.

 **Fish**

How is a fish the **same** as a seal?

_____

How is a fish **different** from a seal?

_____

• • • • • • • • • • • • • • • • • • • •

Birds have feathers. Fish have _____.

Birds have wings. Fish have _____.

Birds fly. Fish _____.

What would a bird-fish look like?
Draw it.

 Fish

Which fish is Fred?
Read the clues.
Make an **X** on the ones that are <u>not</u> Fred.
Then put a **O** around Fred.
Color Fred yellow and blue.

- Fred does <u>not</u> have the biggest tail.

- Fred has spots on his tail.

- Fred does <u>not</u> have sharp teeth.

- Fred does <u>not</u> have a fin on his back.

- Fred is skinny.

 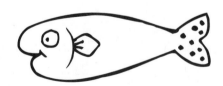 

Name _____

At the Store

What is your favorite thing to buy at the store? _____

Circle the one that does **not** belong.

Fill the shopping bag. Draw items from the list.
Put the heavy things on the bottom.

Shopping List

bread

can of beans

milk

bananas

applesauce

potato chips

At the Store

Write a sentence using the words **store** and **milk**.

_____

_____

Which do you like?
Number the items from 1 to 6.
Your favorite should be number 1.

_____ cereal

_____ bread

_____ fruits and vegetables

_____ frozen foods

_____ chips

_____ candy

Circle the item that you think costs **more**.

What is the **biggest** thing that you can buy at the store?

_____

Critical and Creative Thinking Activities • EMC 3391 • © Evan-Moor Corp.

Dylan and his mom went grocery shopping.
Number the pictures from 1 to 6 to show the correct order.

_____

_____

_____

_____

_____

_____

Write 2 sentences about going grocery shopping.

_____

_____

At the Playground

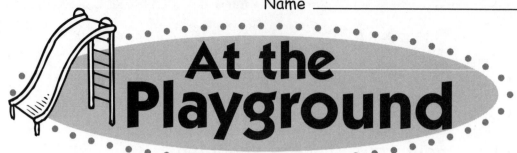

What is your favorite thing to do at the playground?

_____

What is something that you do <u>not</u> like to do at the playground?

_____

Ally and Jake both want to swing.
What can they do?

_____

_____

_____

_____

Write the opposite.

high   _____

fast   _____

Do you notice anything about the words that you wrote?

_____

At the Playground

Put a O around things that you have done at a playground.
Make an X on the things that you have <u>never</u> done at a playground.

crossed a bridge   climbed a ladder

crossed the monkey bars   gone down a slide backwards

slid down a pole   hung upside-down

used a seesaw   pushed someone on a swing

jumped from a high place

What will happen next?

_____

_____

_____

Kylie and her mother walked 6 blocks to the playground.
Kylie played on the swings.
Then they walked home. How far did Kylie walk?

_____ blocks

At the Playground

Fill in the squares. Write the name of each thing that you might find at a playground.

bridge

swing

slide

pole

ladder

sandbox

seesaw

At the Beach

What can you do at the beach?
Write as many things as you can.

1. _____

2. _____

3. _____

4. _____

5. _____

6. _____

7. _____

8. _____

What will happen next?

_____

_____

_____

Number these shells from the smallest to the largest.

____   ____   ____   ____   ____

At the Beach

At the beach...

I see _____.

I hear _____.

I smell _____.

I feel _____.

You are going to the beach.
You can bring <u>only</u> 4 things.
Circle them.

You don't have a pail. What else can you use? _____

You don't have a shovel. What else can you use? _____

At the Beach

The second picture is different from the first picture in 7 ways.
Can you find and circle them all?
Color the picture that you like best.

On the Farm

What are 3 chores that <u>must</u> be done on a farm?

1. _____

2. _____

3. _____

Draw what happens next.

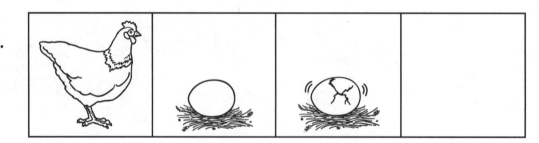

What is the baby called?

chicken _____

cow _____

cat _____

horse _____

goat _____

What would a duck-pig look like? Draw it.

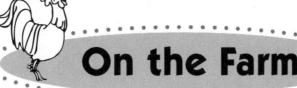

On the Farm

Circle the one that does <u>not</u> belong.

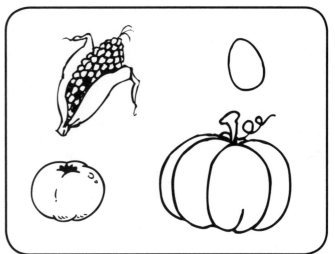

Would you rather ride on a tractor or ride a horse? _____

Why? _____

· · · · · · · · · · · · · · ·

Farmer Fred has 12 chickens.
3 of them are roosters.
How many **hens** does Farmer Fred have?   _____ hens

Farmer Fred collected **4** eggs on Monday,
5 eggs on Tuesday, and **3** eggs on Wednesday.
How many eggs did he collect altogether?   _____ eggs

On the Farm

In each box, draw or write things that can be found on a farm.
Try to put 3 or more things in each box.

Animals	Plants

Buildings	Tools

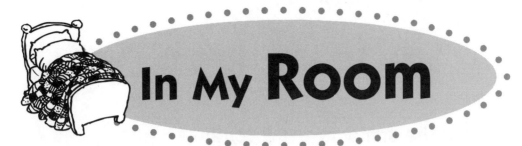

In My Room

Put a **O** around things that are in your room.
Make an **X** on things that are <u>not</u> in your room.

bed	pizza	clock
bowling ball	toys	socks
books	pillow	desk
window	teddy bear	garden

What in your room begins with…

b? _____

s? _____

t? _____

p? _____

c? _____

Draw what you see from a window in your room or in your house.

In My Room

How is your room the **same** as the kitchen?

_____

How is your room **different** from the kitchen?

_____

Circle the 3 words that describe your room best.

cozy	big	noisy
dark	neat	small
cool	messy	cheerful

You are sitting on your bed. Which is closest? Circle it.

the door

the closet

the window

Name these things that can be found in a bedroom.

  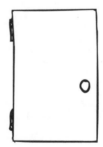 

_____ _____   _____ _____

In My Room

Derek is getting ready for school, but there are a lot of things wrong with his room.
Can you find at least 10? Circle them.
Then draw one more thing that is wrong.

Goldilocks and the Three Bears

What are some things that the bears might have been eating besides porridge?

_____

_____

_____

Write the opposite.

hot _____

big _____

hard _____

asleep _____

Finish the patterns.

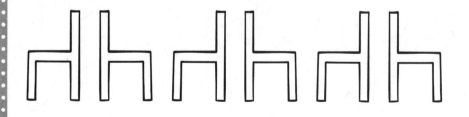

Critical and Creative Thinking Activities • EMC 3391 • © Evan-Moor Corp.

Goldilocks and the Three Bears

How are Goldilocks and Baby Bear the **same**?

_____

How are they **different**?

_____

• • • • • • • • • • • • • • •

Do you think Goldilocks would make a good friend? _____

Why or why not? _____

_____

_____

How did Goldilocks feel when she...

wanted the porridge? _____

broke the chair? _____

felt the beds? _____

saw the bears? _____

Goldilocks and the Three Bears

The second picture is different from the first picture in 8 ways.
Can you find them all? Circle them.
Then add two more things to the second picture.

Name _____

The Three Billy Goats Gruff

Fill in the missing word.

The troll was _____ the bridge.

The goats went _____ the bridge.

The troll was pushed _____ the river.

Write the opposite.

big _____   mean _____

ugly _____   under _____

Color big goats **blue**.
Color medium goats **yellow**.
Color small goats **green**.

The Three Billy Goats Gruff

The sound of the goats on the bridge was "trip, trap, trip, trap." What words could you use for these sounds?

The troll walking on the bridge: _____

Water running under the bridge: _____

The troll falling into the water: _____

Draw the troll.

1. The troll has fur.

2. The troll has horns.

3. The troll has a club.

4. The troll is angry.

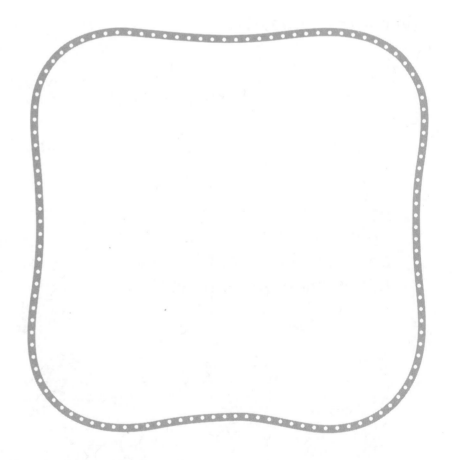

How many horns are on all 3 billy goats? _____

Critical and Creative Thinking Activities • EMC 3391 • © Evan-Moor Corp.

The Three Billy Goats Gruff

Describe each picture with 2 rhyming words.

_____ in a _____

_____ in a _____

_____ on a _____

_____ in a _____

_____ in _____

_____ in _____

The Three Little Pigs

What names would you give to the 3 little pigs?

1. _____ 2. _____ 3. _____

The pigs built their houses from straw, sticks, and bricks. What else could they have used?

_____

_____

_____

Draw one of the pigs' houses.

Fill in the missing words.

Little pig, little _____, let _____ in,

Or I'll _____ and I'll _____ and

I'll _____ your _____ down!

Who said this? _____

The Three Little Pigs

Pigs are pink, wolves are _____.

Pigs have hooves, wolves have _____.

• • • • • • • • • • • • • •

Draw lines to name the pig parts.

snout

ear

hoof

tail

Number the parts of the story in order from 1 to 4.

_____ The wolf could not blow down the house of bricks.

_____ The wolf blew down the house of sticks.

_____ The pigs went off to build their houses.

_____ The wolf blew down the house of straw.

The Three Little Pigs

Help each pig get to its house.
Each pig can move <u>only</u> on its own shape.
Use a different color to show each path.

The Gingerbread Man

Fill in the missing words.

Run, _____ as _____ as _____ can.

You _____ catch _____, I'm

_____ Gingerbread _____!

Why did the Gingerbread Man run away?

_____

• • • • • • • • • • • • • • • •

These are tasty
gingerbread men.

These are <u>not</u> tasty
gingerbread men.

Draw a tasty
gingerbread man.

The Gingerbread Man

Which one does <u>not</u> belong?

SUGAR

Would you eat a talking gingerbread man? _____

Why or why not? _____

Circle the gingerbread man that is different.

The Gingerbread Man

Decorate each gingerbread man differently.

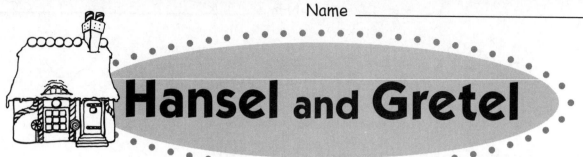

Hansel and Gretel

What would be **good** about having a house made from candy?

_____

_____

What would be **bad** about having a house made from candy?

_____

_____

• • • • • • • • • • • • • • • •

Number the parts of the story in order from 1 to 4.

_____ The children return home to the woodcutter.

_____ The children are lost in the forest.

_____ Gretel pushes the witch into the oven.

_____ Hansel and Gretel find the candy house.

Hansel and Gretel

If the witch's house had been made from vegetables instead of candy, would the children still have come inside?

_____

Why or why not?

_____

_____

_____

Draw a vegetable house.

• • • • • • • • • • • • • •

What kinds of candies would be best for making a...

fence? _____

door? _____

roof? _____

chimney? _____

Hansel and Gretel

The second picture is different from the first picture in 7 ways.
Can you find them all?
Circle them.

Follow the directions to draw and color.

1. Color each roof in a different pattern.

2. Make the trees 3 different colors of green.

3. Draw dots on the big mushrooms.

Cars, Trucks, and Buses

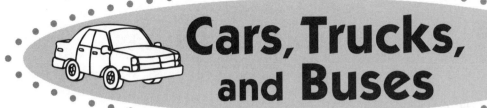

Do you think it would be fun to drive a big cargo truck? _____

Why or why not? _____

What is wrong with this picture?

_____

_____

_____

Match each with what it carries.

 •

 •

 •

How long was your **longest** car trip? _____

Where did you go? _____

Cars, Trucks, and Buses

Can you name 4 different kinds of trucks?

1. _____   3. _____

2. _____   4. _____

Draw what is inside the truck.

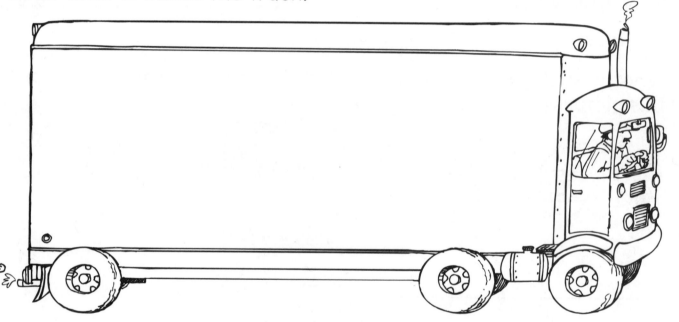

How is a car the **same** as a bus?

_____

How is a car **different** from a bus?

_____

Cars, Trucks, and Buses

Read each numbered item below.
Does it tell about **cars**, **trucks**, **buses**, or **all** of them?
Write the number where it belongs in the Venn diagram.
Make up one of your own for number 10.
Write the number in the diagram.

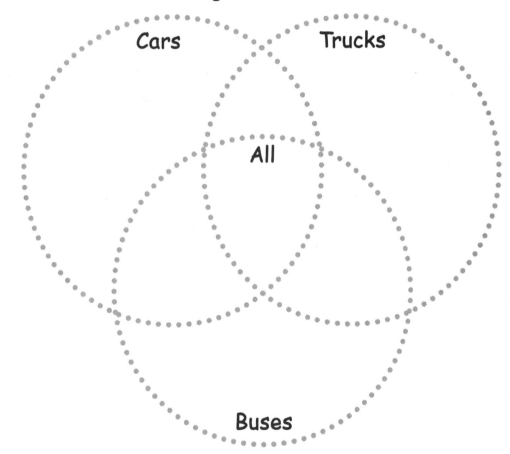

Cars

Trucks

All

Buses

1. carries mostly cargo

2. carries mostly people

3. has the smallest wheels

4. travels on roads

5. has a steering wheel

6. can have more than 4 wheels

7. can go fast

8. has a trunk

9. has a loud horn

10. _____

Would you like to ride in a **motorboat**, a **rowboat**, or a **sailboat**?

_____

Why?

_____

Draw a **sailboat**.
It is on the water.
The sail is red.

Draw a **ship**.
It is gray.
Smoke is coming out.

How are a **boat** and a **ship** different?

_____

 Boats

Would you find a boat in these places?
Write **P** for **probably**.
Write **M** for **maybe**.
Write **N** for **no**.

_____ on the ocean   _____ in the bathtub

_____ in a salt shaker   _____ at a dock

_____ in a bottle   _____ in the desert

_____ on a lake   _____ on a river

Write a sentence using the words **boat** and **lake**.

_____

Finish the pattern.

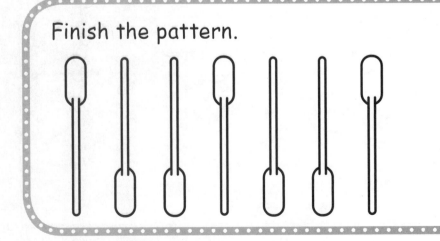

🞐 Boats

The second picture is different from the first picture in 8 ways.
Can you find them all? Circle them.
Draw 2 more differences in the second picture. Color the picture.

All Aboard!

If you could take a train ride, where would you want to go?

_____

How long do you think it would take to get there?

_____

Draw lines to match the cargo to the correct train car.

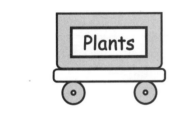  

Would you rather ride in the **engine** or in the **caboose**?

_____

Why? _____

_____

🚂 All Aboard!

You are riding on a train.
What do you see out the window?

In the **country**	At the **station**

Get the train to the station.
Use a **blue** crayon to draw a path that takes the train through 3 tunnels to get to the station.

Use a **red** crayon to draw a path that takes the train through just 1 tunnel to get to the station.

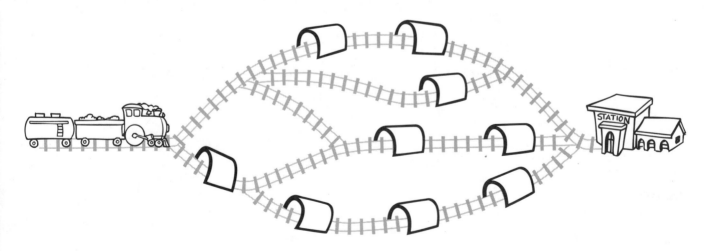

Name _____

All Aboard!

Make five more trains by drawing the shapes in a different order each time.

Planes

Write a sentence that is true about airplanes.

_____

Write a sentence that is <u>not</u> true about airplanes.

_____

· · · · · · · · · · · · · · · · · ·

Which one does <u>not</u> belong?
Write why.

_____

_____

What is wrong with this picture?

_____

_____

_____

What is something else that can fly? _____

Name _____

Planes

How is a plane like a **bird**?

_____

How is a plane like a **train**?

_____

· · · · · · · · · · · · · · · · · ·

Write the opposite.

up   _____

high   _____

fast   _____

take off   _____

You are riding in an airplane. Draw what you **see** out the window.

Where would you like to go on an airplane? Why?

_____

_____

Planes

Put a O around each **airplane** word in the puzzle.

wing	window	tail	seat
cockpit	airport	engine	pilot

```
C  O  C  K  P  I  T  P
S  E  A  T  M  W  R  D
P  W  E  N  G  I  N  E
I  P  T  W  I  N  G  F
L  G  A  X  C  D  Z  R
O  A  I  R  P  O  R  T
T  H  L  Q  K  W  B  V
```

Circle the things that an airplane needs to fly.

engine   seat   wing   window   pilot

Critical and Creative Thinking Activities • EMC 3391 • © Evan-Moor Corp.

Bikes

A car has 4 wheels. A bike has _____ wheels.

A car has a steering wheel. A bike has _____.

In a car, you wear a seat belt.

On a bike, you wear a _____.

• • • • • • • • • • • • • • •

Which picture is different? Circle it.

Circle the things that you have done on a bike.
Cross off the things that you have <u>not</u> done on a bike.

gone down a hill   wiped out

done a "wheelie"   rode on a bike trail

rode through a puddle   rode double

Bikes

Would you like to ride a **bike** or a **scooter?** _____

Why? _____

Tyler rode his bike **4** miles on Saturday.
He rode **3** miles on Sunday.
How many miles did he ride altogether?

_____ miles

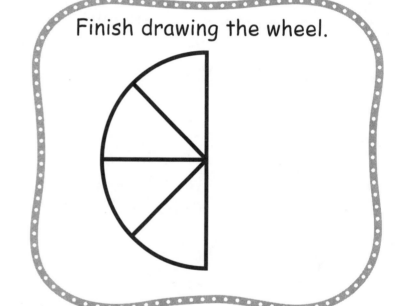

Finish drawing the wheel.

Write a sentence that is true about bikes.

_____

_____

Write a sentence that is <u>not</u> true about bikes.

_____

_____

 **Bikes**

Which bike belongs to Adam?
Read the clues.
Make an **X** on the ones that are <u>not</u> Adam's bike.
Then put a **O** around Adam's bike.

- Adam can ride without training wheels.

- Adam's bike has a flag.

- Adam's bike does <u>not</u> have a basket.

- Adam's bike has a light.

- Adam's bike does <u>not</u> have streamers on the handlebars.

Apples

How does an apple...

look? _____

taste? _____

sound? _____

feel? _____

smell? _____

Which does <u>not</u> belong?

core   seeds

red   skin

Draw an apple tree.
Draw 8 apples on the tree.
Draw 4 apples on the ground.
Draw a basket next to
the tree.

Finish the pattern.

 Apples

What is another food that...

is red? _____

is round? _____

grows on a tree? _____

begins with **A**? _____

What can you make out of apples?

apple _____   apple _____

apple _____   apple _____

How many apples should be in the last bag? Draw them.

Write a sentence using the words **apple** and **tree**.

_____

_____

🍎 Apples

Morgan and her mom are making an apple pie.
Number the pictures from 1 to 6 to show the correct order.

_____

_____

_____

_____

_____

_____

On the back, write or draw what <u>you</u> would like to put in a pie.

Trees

Can you think of 4 different kinds of trees?

1. _____   3. _____

2. _____   4. _____

What lives in this tree?
Draw 3 different animals
in the box.

Would you like to live in a treehouse? _____

Why or why not? _____

Name _____

Trees

You are in a tree.
What do you...

see? _____

hear? _____

feel? _____

smell? _____

Circle things that **grow** on trees.

Draw lines to match.

pine tree •

oak tree •

palm tree •

Trees

Help the squirrel get to its stash of nuts.
Be sure not to run into any other animals!

Name _____

Water

Can you think of 4 different ways to use water?

1. _____ 3. _____

2. _____ 4. _____

What words rhyme with **rain**?

_____ _____

_____ _____

Which one does <u>not</u> belong? Circle it.

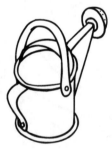   

Write a sentence using the words **water** and **bath**.

_____

_____

Critical and Creative Thinking Activities • EMC 3391 • © Evan-Moor Corp.

Water

Can you think of 4 different places where water is found outside?

1. _____

2. _____

3. _____

4. _____

Read each numbered item below.
Does it tell about a **swimming pool**, a **lake**, or **both**?
Write the number where it belongs in the Venn diagram.

1. land all around

2. cement bottom

3. has plants and fish

4. people ride in boats

5. can swim in it

6. have to clean it

7. in a backyard

8. can't see the bottom

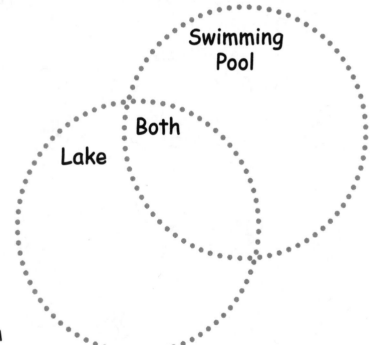

Would you rather swim in a **swimming pool** or in a **lake**? Why?

_____

_____

💧 Water

Color the raindrops with **even numbers** red.

What do you see? _____

 Critical and Creative Thinking Activities • EMC 3391 • © Evan-Moor Corp.

Crayons

Color these crayons with your 3 favorite colors.

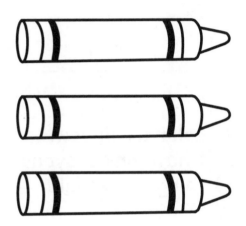

Draw a picture. Use your 3 favorite colors.

What do you think would happen to your crayons if you…

left them in the sun? _____

dropped a book on them? _____

put them in water? _____

Finish the pattern.

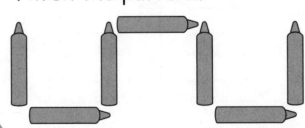

Crayons

How is a crayon the **same** as a pencil?

_____

How is a crayon **different** from a pencil?

_____

How many crayons will fit in the box?

_____

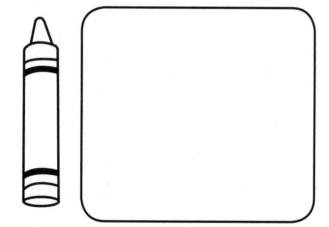

You want to color a rainbow, but you don't have any crayons. What are 3 things you could use instead?

1. _____

2. _____

3. _____

Look at the pattern. Fill in the missing crayons.

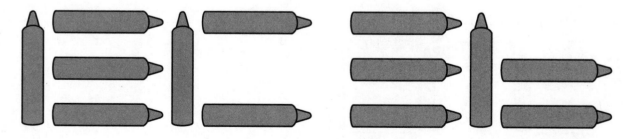

Crayons

Fill in the squares.
Write the name of the color that goes with each clue.
Then color the tip of the crayon with the correct color.

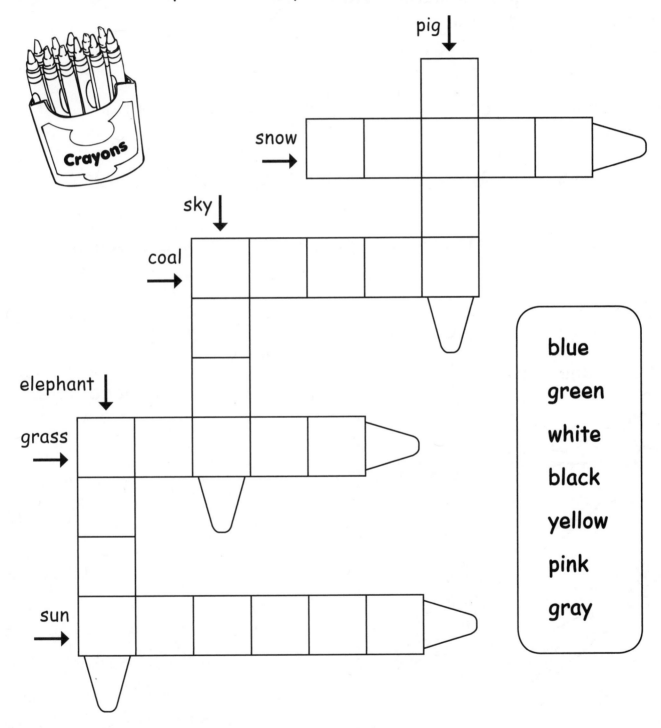

pig ↓

snow →

sky ↓

coal →

elephant ↓

grass →

sun →

blue

green

white

black

yellow

pink

gray

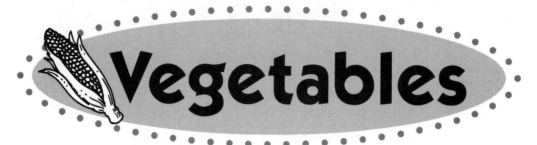

Vegetables

There are so many kinds of vegetables!
Draw a line under the ones that you have tried.
Circle the ones that you like.

corn	carrots	zucchini	cucumber
celery	broccoli	asparagus	cauliflower
peas	lettuce	potatoes	green beans

Which one does <u>not</u> belong?

Draw your favorite vegetable.

Vegetables

Which do you like?
Number the vegetables
from 1 to 6.
The one you like the most
should be number 1.

_____ peas

_____ spinach

_____ carrots

_____ corn

_____ green beans

_____ celery

What is a vegetable
that you do <u>not</u> like?

_____

Draw a head using <u>only</u> vegetables.

What vegetables did you use?

eyes: _____

nose: _____

mouth: _____

ears: _____

hair: _____

Vegetables

Read the clues to find the mystery vegetables!

I am **orange**.
Rabbits like me.
I grow underground.

I am a _____.

I am **green**.
I am in most salads.
You eat my leaves.

I am _____.

I am **green**.
I am used to make pickles.
I start with **C**.

I am a _____.

We are **green**.
We are small and round.
We grow in a pod.

We are _____.

I am **yellow**.
I grow on a stalk.
You can eat me off the cob.

I am _____.

I am **brown** on the outside.
I am **white** on the inside.
I grow underground.

I am a _____.

Shirts

Write 4 words about the shirt that you are wearing right now, or about your favorite shirt.

1. _____   3. _____

2. _____   4. _____

Draw to make the shirts different in 3 ways.

Ryan has 3 blue shirts and 6 red shirts.
He also has a yellow shirt.
How many shirts does Ryan have?

_____ shirts

Lindsey had 9 shirts.
She gave 3 shirts to her little sister.
How many shirts does Lindsey have now?

_____ shirts

How many holes does this shirt have?

_____

Name _____

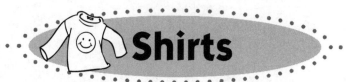

Shirts

How is a shirt the **same** as a jacket?

_____

How is a shirt **different** from a jacket?

_____

What would a shirt for an octopus look like? Draw it in the box.

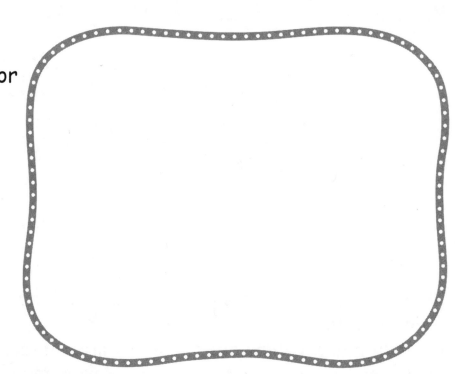

Do you have any shirts that are...

too big? _____   too small? _____

itchy? _____   torn? _____

faded? _____   for a sport? _____

 **Shirts**

Look at each picture below.
Does the shirt have **stripes**, **long sleeves**, or **both**?
Write the number where it belongs in the Venn diagram.

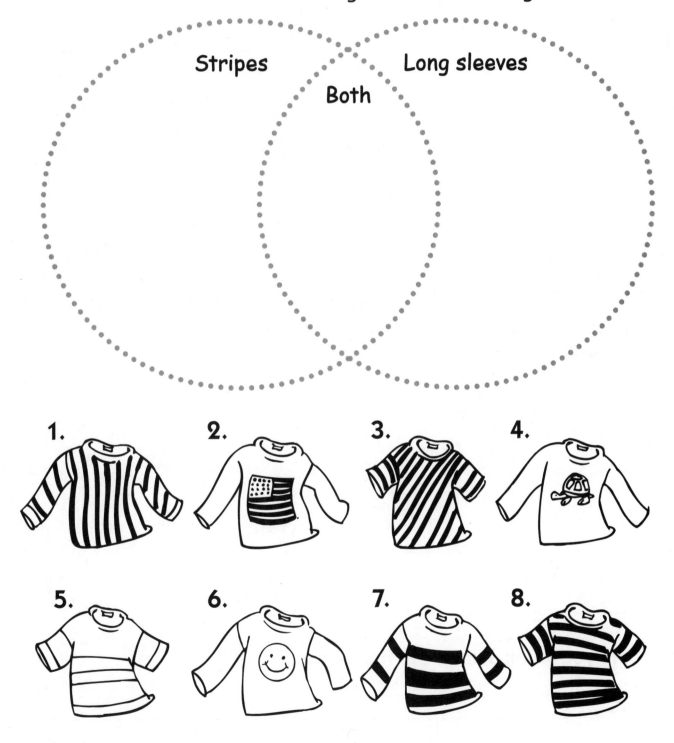

Hats

What are 3 reasons why people wear hats?

1. _____

2. _____

3. _____

What is wrong with
this picture?

_____

_____

It is Silly Hat Day.
Draw the silliest hat that
you can!

Why do you think some hats have brims?

_____

Hats

You can wear a hat.
What else can you use a hat for?

_____

These are Happy Hats.

These are <u>not</u> Happy Hats.

Circle the Happy Hat.

Color each party hat differently.
Use <u>only</u> 4 colors.

Hats

Who would wear each of these hats?

Critical and Creative Thinking Activities • EMC 3391 • © Evan-Moor Corp.

Ice Cream

What is your **favorite** flavor of ice cream? _____

Do you like it in a **cone** or in a **dish**? _____

You are making an ice-cream sundae.
Circle the things that you will use.

Draw your sundae.

Write a sentence using the words **ice cream** and **melt**.

_____

_____

Ice Cream

How many **different** flavors of
ice cream can you think of?

1. _____

2. _____

3. _____

4. _____

5. _____

6. _____

7. _____

8. _____

Which does <u>not</u> belong? Circle it.

It is a hot day.
Your cone is dripping.
What can you do?

_____

_____

Which bowl of ice cream is different? Circle it.

Ice Cream

Which ice-cream treat did Anna eat?
Read the clues.
Make an **X** on the ones that are <u>not</u> Anna's treat.
Then put a **O** around Anna's treat.

- Anna got only one scoop of ice cream.

- Anna does <u>not</u> like cherries.

- Anna's ice cream is <u>not</u> in a dish.

- Anna got sprinkles on her ice cream.

Shapes

Write a sentence using the words **paper** and **rectangle**.

_____

_____

What is a shape with no corners? _____

Here are the tops of some shapes.
The bottoms are just the same.
Draw the bottom of each shape.

Shapes

How many triangles? _____

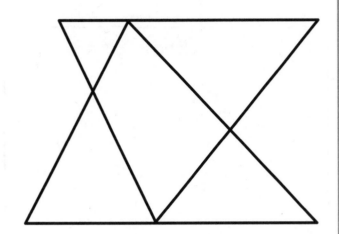

How many circles? _____

What is something that is...

small and round? _____

big and round? _____

small and rectangular? _____

big and rectangular? _____

How many corners do **2 triangles** have? _____

How many corners do **2 squares** have? _____

How many corners do **1 triangle** and **1 square** have? _____

Shapes

Draw the things listed below using <u>only</u> 3 shapes:
triangles △, rectangles ▭, and circles ○.

House	Boat

Cat	Person

Shoes and Socks

Don't look!
What color are your socks?

_____

What color are the bottoms of
your shoes?

_____

What size shoe do you wear?

_____

Draw the other sock.

Color them the same.

What size shoe do you think you will wear when you are grown up?

_____

How are shoes the **same** as socks?

_____

How are shoes **different** from socks?

_____

Shoes and Socks

What kind of shoes can you wear...

in the rain? _____

at the beach? _____

playing soccer? _____

Emily has 8 socks.
How many **pairs** of socks does she have?

_____ pairs of socks

Darrin has 3 pairs of socks.
How many **socks** does he have?

_____ socks

Draw lines to match the shoes and socks.

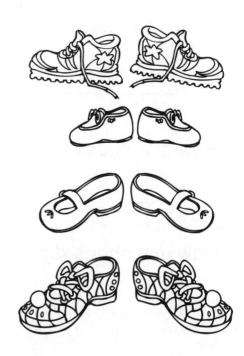

Shoes and Socks
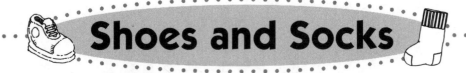

Find the matching shoes.
Color them the same.

My Family

How many people are in your family? _____

Who is the **youngest** person in your family? _____

Who is the **oldest** person in your family? _____

You want to make sure that each person in your family gets an equal slice of this pizza.
Draw lines to show the slices.

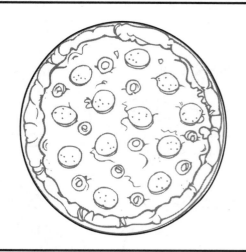

Circle who you are in your family.

daughter   brother   niece

grandchild   sister   nephew

son   cousin   helper

My Family

Your mother's mother is your _____.

Your father's sister is your _____.

What do you think is the hardest thing about being a **child**?

_____

_____

What do you think is the hardest thing about being a **parent**?

_____

_____

Draw 3 things that are important to your family.

My Family

Read the list of things to do with your family.
Where do you do each thing?
Outside, **inside**, or **both**?
Write the number where it belongs in the Venn diagram.

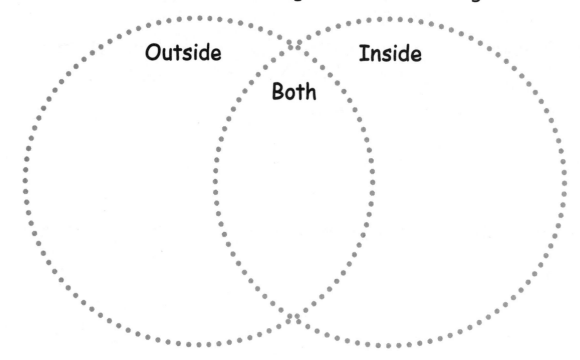

Outside   Inside

Both

1. Go to the park.   **6.** Go to the zoo.

2. Go on a picnic.   **7.** Play a board game.

3. Eat dinner.   **8.** Take a walk.

4. Fly a kite.   **9.** Make cookies.

5. Watch TV.   **10.** Play music.

Which is your **favorite** thing to do? _____

Answer Key

Many of the questions in this book are open-ended, and students' answers will vary. Sample responses are provided for most of these activities. Accept any reasonable responses.

Page 5

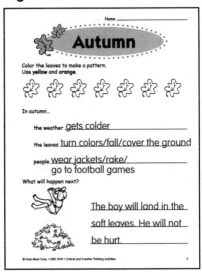

Page 6

Page 7

Page 8

Page 9

Page 10

Page 11

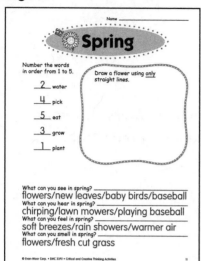

Spring

Number the words in order from 1 to 5.

2 water
4 pick
5 eat
3 grow
1 plant

Draw a flower using only straight lines.

What can you see in spring?
flowers/new leaves/baby birds/baseball
What can you hear in spring?
chirping/lawn mowers/playing baseball
What can you feel in spring?
soft breezes/rain showers/warmer air
What can you smell in spring?
flowers/fresh cut grass

Page 12

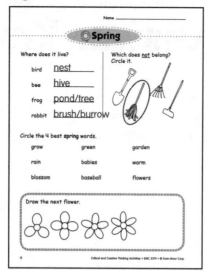

Spring

Where does it live?

bird   nest
bee   hive
frog   pond/tree
rabbit brush/burrow

Which does not belong? Circle it.

Circle the 4 best spring words.

grow   green   garden
rain   babies   warm
blossom   baseball   flowers

Draw the next flower.

Page 13

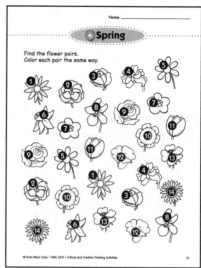

Spring

Find the flower pairs. Color each pair the same way.

Page 14

Summer

What do you like to do?
Number the activities from 1 to 6.
The one you like the most should be number 1.

____ hiking   ____ riding a bike
____ swimming   ____ having a picnic
____ climbing trees ____ going to the zoo

Write the opposite.

sunny   cloudy/rainy
hot   cold
wet   dry
play   rest/work

You made lemonade.
How many glasses do you think you can fill?

____ glasses of lemonade

Page 15

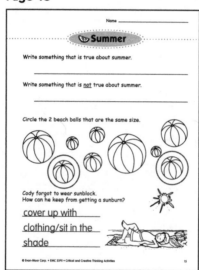

Summer

Write something that is true about summer.

_____

Write something that is not true about summer.

_____

Circle the 2 beach balls that are the same size.

Cody forgot to wear sunblock.
How can he keep from getting a sunburn?

cover up with
clothing/sit in the
shade

Page 16

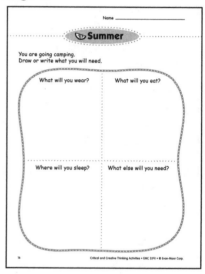

Summer

You are going camping.
Draw or write what you will need.

| What will you wear? | What will you eat? |
| Where will you sleep? | What else will you need? |

Page 17

Halloween

What are 3 things that scare you?

1. _____
2. _____
3. _____

What scares other people but does not scare you?

_____

Jenna grew 6 big pumpkins and 3 small pumpkins in her garden.
How many pumpkins did Jenna grow altogether?

9 pumpkins

Draw the jack-o'-lantern upside down.

Page 18

Halloween

Circle the things that you might do at a Halloween party.
Cross off the things that you would not do at a Halloween party.

bob for apples   eat candy   wear a costume
hunt for eggs   open presents   carve a pumpkin

Circle the one that does not belong. Tell someone why.

Finish the pattern.

Page 19

Halloween

Follow the directions to make a Halloween picture.

1. Draw a ghost in the middle window.
2. Draw a different jack-o'-lantern in each corner window.
3. Draw a black cat in the window below the ghost.
4. Draw a spider web in the window above the ghost.
5. Draw something spooky in the last 2 windows.

Answers will Vary

Page 20

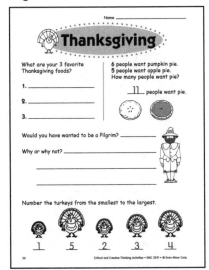

Name _____

Thanksgiving

What are your 3 favorite Thanksgiving foods?

1. _____
2. _____
3. _____

6 people want pumpkin pie.
5 people want apple pie.
How many people want pie?

11 people want pie.

Would you have wanted to be a Pilgrim? _____

Why or why not? _____
_____
_____

Number the turkeys from the smallest to the largest.

1   5   3   2   4

Page 21

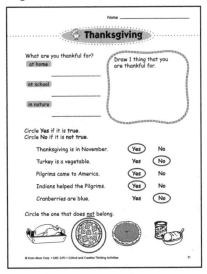

Name _____

Thanksgiving

What are you thankful for?

at home _____

at school _____

in nature _____

Draw 1 thing that you are thankful for.

Circle **Yes** if it is true.
Circle **No** if it is not true.

Thanksgiving is in November.   (Yes)   No
Turkey is a vegetable.   Yes   (No)
Pilgrims came to America.   (Yes)   No
Indians helped the Pilgrims.   (Yes)   No
Cranberries are blue.   Yes   (No)

Circle the one that does *not* belong.

Page 22

Name _____

Thanksgiving

Color each turkey differently.
Use only brown, red, yellow, and orange.

How many times did you use **brown**? _____
How many times did you use **red**? _____
How many times did you use **yellow**? _____
How many times did you use **orange**? _____

Page 23

Name _____

Christmas

On Christmas, what do you...

see? _____
hear? _____
feel? _____
smell? _____
taste? _____

Color each pair of bells differently.

Page 24

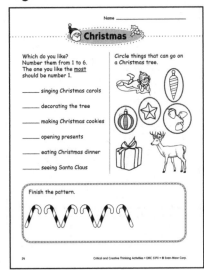

Name _____

Christmas

Which do you like?
Number them from 1 to 6.
The one you like the *most* should be number 1.

____ singing Christmas carols
____ decorating the tree
____ making Christmas cookies
____ opening presents
____ eating Christmas dinner
____ seeing Santa Claus

Circle things that can go on a Christmas tree.

Finish the pattern.

Page 25

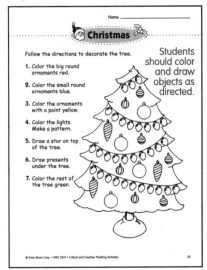

Name _____

Christmas

Follow the directions to decorate the tree.

1. Color the big round ornaments red.
2. Color the small round ornaments blue.
3. Color the ornaments with a point yellow.
4. Color the lights. Make a pattern.
5. Draw a star on top of the tree.
6. Draw presents under the tree.
7. Color the rest of the tree green.

Students should color and draw objects as directed.

Page 26

Name _____

Hanukkah

How many days is Hanukkah? **8**

Draw 9 candles on the menorah. Use yellow and blue. Make a pattern.

Draw each Hebrew letter on one of the dreidels.

Number the dreidels in order from the smallest to the largest.

5   3   2   4   1

Page 27

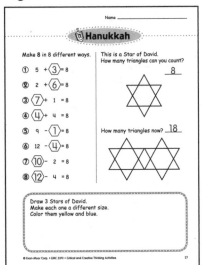

Name _____

Hanukkah

Make 8 in 8 different ways.

① 5 + (3) = 8
② 2 + (6) = 8
③ (7) + 1 = 8
④ (4) + 4 = 8
⑤ 9 - (1) = 8
⑥ 12 - (4) = 8
⑦ (10) - 2 = 8
⑧ (12) - 4 = 8

This is a Star of David.
How many triangles can you count?   **8**

How many triangles now?   **18**

Draw 3 Stars of David.
Make each one a different size.
Color them yellow and blue.

Page 28

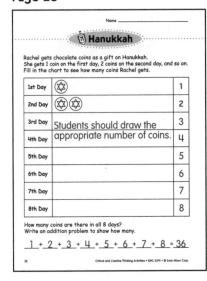

Name _____

Hanukkah

Rachel gets chocolate coins as a gift on Hanukkah.
She gets 1 coin on the first day, 2 coins on the second day, and so on.
Fill in the chart to see how many coins Rachel gets.

1st Day	✡	1
2nd Day	✡ ✡	2
3rd Day		3
4th Day	Students should draw the appropriate number of coins.	4
5th Day		5
6th Day		6
7th Day		7
8th Day		8

How many coins are there in all 8 days?
Write an addition problem to show how many.

__1__ + __2__ + __3__ + __4__ + __5__ + __6__ + __7__ + __8__ = __36__

Page 29

Name _____

Valentine's Day

Finish each sentence differently.

I love _____

I love _____

I love _____

3 hearts are the same size.
Color them.

What is something that is usually **pink**? _____

What is something that is always **red**? _____

What is something that is always **white**? _____

Page 30

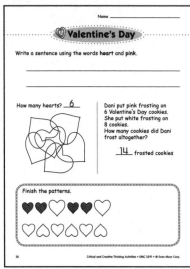

Name _____

Valentine's Day

Write a sentence using the words **heart** and **pink**.

_____

_____

How many hearts? _6_

Dani put pink frosting on 6 Valentine's Day cookies. She put white frosting on 8 cookies. How many cookies did Dani frost altogether?

_14_ frosted cookies

Finish the patterns.

Page 31

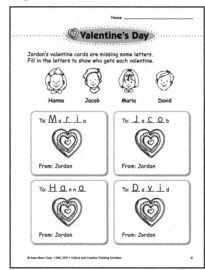

Name _____

Valentine's Day

Jordon's valentine cards are missing some letters.
Fill in the letters to show who gets each valentine.

Hanna   Jacob   Maria   David

To: M a r i a
From: Jordon

To: J a c o b
From: Jordon

To: H a n n a
From: Jordon

To: D a v i d
From: Jordon

Page 32

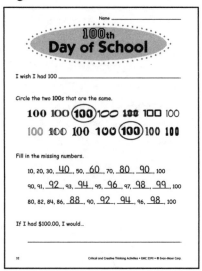

Name _____

100th Day of School

I wish I had 100 _____

Circle the two 100s that are the same.

100 100 (100) 100 100 100 100

100 100 100 100 (100) 100 100

Fill in the missing numbers.

10, 20, 30, _40_, 50, _60_, 70, _80_, _90_, 100

90, 91, _92_, 93, _94_, 95, _96_, 97, _98_, _99_, 100

80, 82, 84, 86, _88_, 90, _92_, _94_, 96, _98_, 100

If I had $100.00, I would…

_____

Page 33

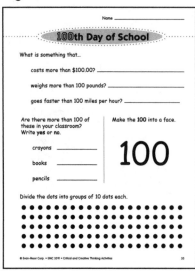

Name _____

100th Day of School

What is something that…

costs more than $100.00? _____

weighs more than 100 pounds? _____

goes faster than 100 miles per hour? _____

Are there more than 100 of these in your classroom?
Write **yes** or **no**.

crayons _____

books _____

pencils _____

Make the 100 into a face.

100

Divide the dots into groups of 10 dots each.

Page 34

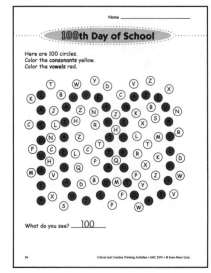

Name _____

100th Day of School

Here are 100 circles.
Color the **consonants** yellow.
Color the **vowels** red.

What do you see? _100_

Page 35

Name _____

Cats and Dogs

Which do you like better, **cats** or **dogs**? _____

Why? _____

Write 3 words that describe cats.

1. _____
2. _____
3. _____

Which does **not** belong?

Write 3 **different** words that describe **dogs**.

1. _____
2. _____
3. _____

Page 36

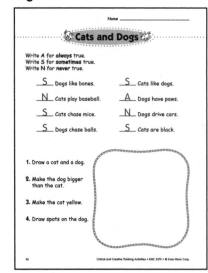

Name _____

Cats and Dogs

Write **A** for **always** true.
Write **S** for **sometimes** true.
Write **N** for **never** true.

_S_ Dogs like bones.   _S_ Cats like dogs.

_N_ Cats play baseball.   _A_ Dogs have paws.

_S_ Cats chase mice.   _N_ Dogs drive cars.

_S_ Dogs chase balls.   _S_ Cats are black.

1. Draw a cat and a dog.
2. Make the dog bigger than the cat.
3. Make the cat yellow.
4. Draw spots on the dog.

Page 37

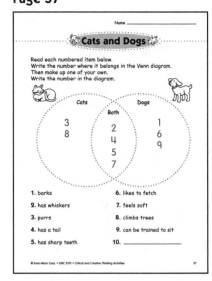

Name _____

Cats and Dogs

Read each numbered item below.
Write the number where it belongs in the Venn diagram.
Then make up one of your own.
Write the number in the diagram.

Cats   Both   Dogs

3
8   2
         4   1
         5   6
         7   9

1. barks   6. likes to fetch
2. has whiskers   7. feels soft
3. purrs   8. climbs trees
4. has a tail   9. can be trained to sit
5. has sharp teeth   10. _____

Critical and Creative Thinking Activities • EMC 3391 • © Evan-Moor Corp.

Page 38

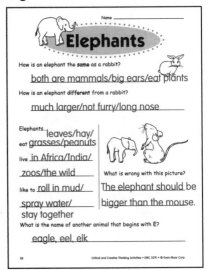

Name _____

Elephants

How is an elephant the **same** as a rabbit?

both are mammals/big ears/eat plants

How is an elephant **different** from a rabbit?

much larger/not furry/long nose

Elephants...
eat leaves/hay/grasses/peanuts

live in Africa/India/zoos/the wild

like to roll in mud/spray water/stay together

What is wrong with this picture?

The elephant should be bigger than the mouse.

What is the name of another animal that begins with E?

eagle, eel, elk

Page 39

Name _____

Elephants

What would be **fun** about having an elephant for a pet?

_____

Why would it be **hard** to have an elephant for a pet?

_____

What is another animal that...

is big? giraffe   has rough skin? lizard

is gray? mouse   has tusks? boar/walrus/warthog

Circle the elephant that is different.

Page 40

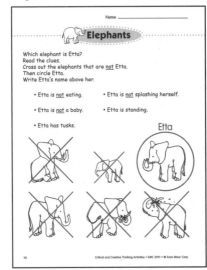

Name _____

Elephants

Which elephant is Etta?
Read the clues.
Cross out the elephants that are **not** Etta.
Then circle Etta.
Write Etta's name above her.

- Etta is **not** eating.
- Etta is **not** splashing herself.
- Etta is **not** a baby.
- Etta is standing.
- Etta has tusks.

Etta

Page 41

Name _____

Lions

Write a sentence that is true about lions.

_____

Write a sentence that is **not** true about lions.

_____

What is another animal that...

hunts for meat? _____

lives in Africa? _____

has babies called cubs? wolves/bears

Which lion is different?   nose and tail

Write a sentence about lions using the words **cubs** and **hunt**.

_____

Page 42

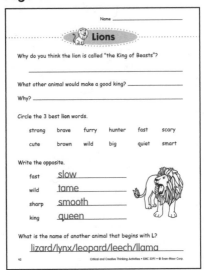

Name _____

Lions

Why do you think the lion is called "the King of Beasts"?

_____

What other animal would make a good king? _____

Why? _____

Circle the 3 best lion words.

strong   brave   furry   hunter   fast   scary

cute   brown   wild   big   quiet   smart

Write the opposite.

fast   slow

wild   tame

sharp   smooth

king   queen

What is the name of another animal that begins with L?

lizard/lynx/leopard/leech/llama

Page 43

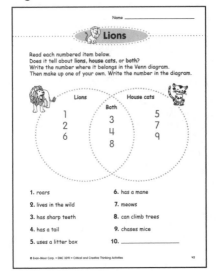

Name _____

Lions

Read each numbered item below.
Does it tell about **lions**, **house cats**, or **both**?
Write the number where it belongs in the Venn diagram.
Then make up one of your own. Write the number in the diagram.

Lions: 1 2 6
Both: 3 4 8
House cats: 5 7 9

1. roars
2. lives in the wild
3. has sharp teeth
4. has a tail
5. uses a litter box
6. has a mane
7. meows
8. can climb trees
9. chases mice
10. _____

Page 44

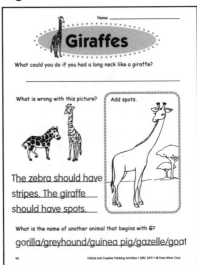

Name _____

Giraffes

What could you do if you had a long neck like a giraffe?

_____

What is wrong with this picture?   Add spots.

The zebra should have stripes. The giraffe should have spots.

What is the name of another animal that begins with G?

gorilla/greyhound/guinea pig/gazelle/goat

Page 45

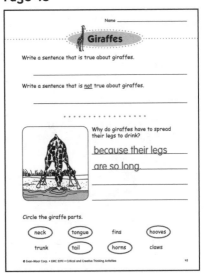

Name _____

Giraffes

Write a sentence that is true about giraffes.

_____

Write a sentence that is **not** true about giraffes.

_____

Why do giraffes have to spread their legs to drink?

because their legs are so long

Circle the giraffe parts.

neck   tongue   fins   hooves

trunk   tail   horns   claws

Page 46

Name _____

Giraffes

Look at the animals in each row.
Then write why they belong together.

run fast

long necks

horns/eat plants

Page 47

Kangaroos

Kangaroos hop.
What are 2 other animals that hop?

rabbits and _frogs_

Kangaroos eat grass.
What are 2 other animals that eat grass?

rabbits and _deer_

How many joeys? _2_

How many kangaroos? _4_

How many ears? _8_

A baby kangaroo is called a **joey**.
Add a joey in the pouch.

Page 48

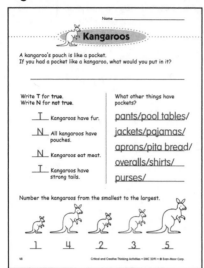

Kangaroos

A kangaroo's pouch is like a pocket.
If you had a pocket like a kangaroo, what would you put in it?

_____

Write T for **true**.
Write N for **not true**.

_T_ Kangaroos have fur.

_N_ All kangaroos have pouches.

_N_ Kangaroos eat meat.

_T_ Kangaroos have strong tails.

What other things have pockets?

pants/pool tables/
jackets/pajamas/
aprons/pita bread/
overalls/shirts/
purses/

Number the kangaroos from the smallest to the largest.

_1_   _4_   _2_   _3_   _5_

Page 49

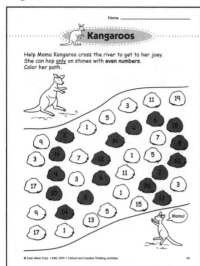

Kangaroos

Help Mama Kangaroo cross the river to get to her joey.
She can hop **only** on stones with **even numbers**.
Color her path.

Page 50

Bears

How is a real bear the **same** as a teddy bear?

Has 4 legs/looks sort of like a bear

How is a real bear **different** from a teddy bear?

is alive/has fur/not fabric/has teeth/can't
hold it/can live in a zoo

Can you think of 3 different kinds of bears?

1. brown
2. grizzly
3. black

Write 3 words that rhyme with **bear**.

1. hair
2. scare
3. fair

Color the bears. Make a pattern.
Use **only** black and brown.

Page 51

Bears

What do bears eat?
Draw or write as many things as you can.

grass/mushrooms/insects/leaves/
berries/fish/flowers/nuts/honey

Mama Bear ate 6 fish.
Her 2 cubs ate 3 fish each.
How many fish did the bears eat altogether?

_12_ fish

Which of these prints was made by a bear? Circle it.

Finish each sentence.

Bears like _____

Bears need _____

Bears have _____

Page 52

Bears

What is wrong with this picture?
Try to find at least 10 things.
Color them.

Page 53

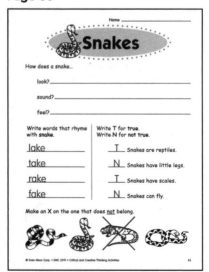

Snakes

How does a snake...

look? _____

sound? _____

feel? _____

Write words that rhyme with **snake**.

lake
take
rake
fake

Write T for **true**.
Write N for **not true**.

_T_ Snakes are reptiles.

_N_ Snakes have little legs.

_T_ Snakes have scales.

_N_ Snakes can fly.

Make an X on the one that does **not** belong.

Page 54

Snakes

Would you like to have a snake for a pet?

Why or why not? _____

Color the snake's stripes.
Use this pattern: **ABABC**.

Write the opposite.

long _short_   skinny _fat_

cold _hot_   dangerous _safe_

Page 55

Snakes

These 4 snakes are all tangled up.
Color each snake a different color.

Make the word **SNAKE** with snakes!
Draw snakes to make the missing letters.

Letters are **N** and **E**. Drawings will vary.

Page 56

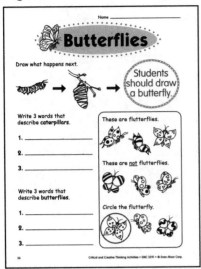

Butterflies

Name _____

Draw what happens next.

Students should draw a butterfly.

Write 3 words that describe **caterpillars**.

1. _____
2. _____
3. _____

Write 3 words that describe **butterflies**.

1. _____
2. _____
3. _____

These are flutterflies.

These are **not** flutterflies.

Circle the flutterfly.

Page 57

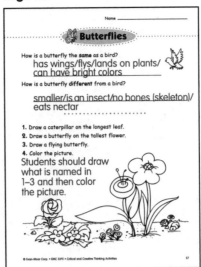

Butterflies

Name _____

How is a butterfly the **same** as a bird?
has wings/flys/lands on plants/ can have bright colors

How is a butterfly **different** from a bird?
smaller/is an insect/no bones (skeleton)/ eats nectar

1. Draw a caterpillar on the longest leaf.
2. Draw a butterfly on the tallest flower.
3. Draw a flying butterfly.
4. Color the picture.
Students should draw what is named in 1–3 and then color the picture.

Page 58

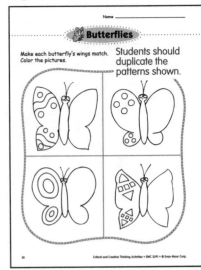

Butterflies

Name _____

Make each butterfly's wings match. Color the pictures.

Students should duplicate the patterns shown.

Page 59

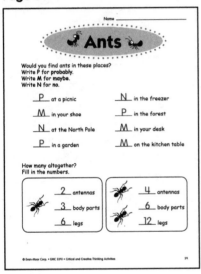

Ants

Name _____

Would you find ants in these places?
Write **P** for probably.
Write **M** for maybe.
Write **N** for no.

P at a picnic
M in your shoe
N at the North Pole
P in a garden

N in the freezer
P in the forest
P in your desk
M on the kitchen table

How many altogether?
Fill in the numbers.

2 antennas
3 body parts
6 legs

4 antennas
6 body parts
12 legs

Page 60

Ants

Name _____

You find an ant on your **sandwich**. What do you do?

_____

You find an ant in your **juice**. What do you do?

_____

Which ant is different?

Put a O around the first ant.
Draw a ☐ around the last ant.
Make an X on the middle ant.

How many ants do you think could fit on a penny?

_____ ants

Circle the 4 best **ant** words.

small   cute   insect   icky

busy   strong   quick   brave

Page 61

Ants

Name _____

Help Alvin Ant collect as many crumbs as he can on his way back to the anthill.
Draw a path.
Try to get at least 15 crumbs.

One possible path is shown.

How many crumbs did Alvin get? _____

Page 62

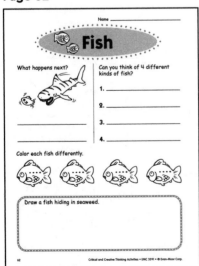

Fish

Name _____

What happens next?

Can you think of 4 different kinds of fish?

1. _____
2. _____
3. _____
4. _____

Color each fish differently.

Draw a fish hiding in seaweed.

Page 63

Fish

Name _____

How is a fish the **same** as a seal?
swims/lives in ocean/has fins

How is a fish **different** from a seal?
breathes under water/ has scales/no fur/lays eggs

Birds have feathers. Fish have scales

Birds have wings. Fish have fins

Birds fly. Fish swim

What would a bird-fish look like?
Draw it.

Page 64

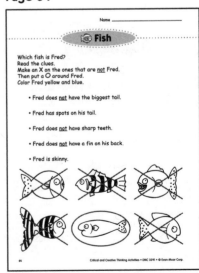

Fish

Name _____

Which fish is Fred?
Read the clues.
Make an X on the ones that are **not** Fred.
Then put a O around Fred.
Color Fred yellow and blue.

• Fred does **not** have the biggest tail.

• Fred has spots on his tail.

• Fred does **not** have sharp teeth.

• Fred does **not** have a fin on his back.

• Fred is skinny.

Page 65

Name _____

At the Store

What is your favorite thing to buy at the store? _____

Circle the one that does not belong.

Fill the shopping bag. Draw items from the list.
Put the heavy things on the bottom.

Shopping List
bread
can of beans
milk
bananas
applesauce
potato chips

Page 66

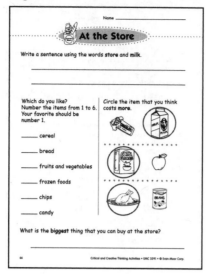

Name _____

At the Store

Write a sentence using the words **store** and **milk**.

Which do you like?
Number the items from 1 to 6.
Your favorite should be number 1.

_____ cereal
_____ bread
_____ fruits and vegetables
_____ frozen foods
_____ chips
_____ candy

Circle the item that you think costs **more**.

What is the **biggest** thing that you can buy at the store?

Page 67

Name _____

At the Store

Dylan and his mom went grocery shopping.
Number the pictures from 1 to 6 to show the correct order.

5 4 2
1 6 3

Write 2 sentences about going grocery shopping.

Page 68

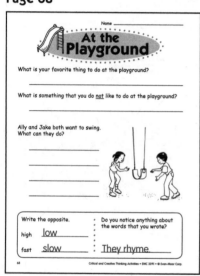

Name _____

At the Playground

What is your favorite thing to do at the playground?

_____

What is something that you do not like to do at the playground?

_____

Ally and Jake both want to swing.
What can they do?

_____

Write the opposite.

high   low
fast   slow

Do you notice anything about the words that you wrote?

They rhyme.

Page 69

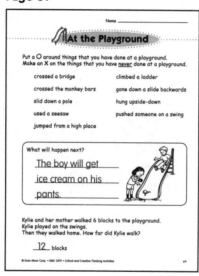

Name _____

At the Playground

Put a O around things that you have done at a playground.
Make an X on the things that you have never done at a playground.

crossed a bridge
crossed the monkey bars
slid down a pole
used a seesaw
jumped from a high place

climbed a ladder
gone down a slide backwards
hung upside-down
pushed someone on a swing

What will happen next?

The boy will get ice cream on his pants.

Kylie and her mother walked 6 blocks to the playground.
Kylie played on the swings.
Then they walked home. How far did Kylie walk?

12 blocks

Page 70

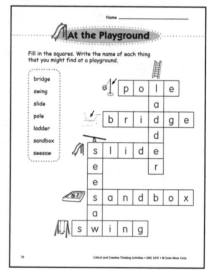

Name _____

At the Playground

Fill in the squares. Write the name of each thing that you might find at a playground.

bridge
swing
slide
pole
ladder
sandbox
seesaw

p o l e
a
b r i d g e
d
s l i d e
e   r
e
s a n d b o x
a
s w i n g

Page 71

Name _____

At the Beach

What can you do at the beach?
Write as many things as you can.

1. lie in the sun
2. build a sand castle
3. wade in water
4. play volleyball
5. look in tide pools
6. dig holes in water
7. boogie board
8. surf

What will happen next?

The waves will wash away the sand castle.

Number these shells from the smallest to the largest.

3 1 2 4 5

Page 72

Name _____

At the Beach

At the beach...

I see _____
I hear _____
I smell _____
I feel _____

You are going to the beach.
You can bring only 4 things.
Circle them.

You don't have a pail. What else can you use? _____

You don't have a shovel. What else can you use? _____

Page 73

Name _____

At the Beach

The second picture is different from the first picture in 7 ways.
Can you find and circle them all?
Color the picture that you like best.

Critical and Creative Thinking Activities • EMC 3391 • © Evan-Moor Corp.

Page 74

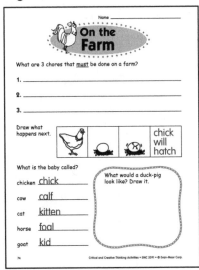

Name _____

On the Farm

What are 3 chores that <u>must</u> be done on a farm?

1. _____
2. _____
3. _____

Draw what happens next.

| 🐔 | 🥚 | 🐣 | chick will hatch |

What is the baby called?

chicken chick

cow calf

cat kitten

horse foal

goat kid

What would a duck-pig look like? Draw it.

<small>74   Critical and Creative Thinking Activities • EMC 3391 • © Evan-Moor Corp.</small>

Page 75

Name _____

On the Farm

Circle the one that does not belong.

Would you rather ride on a tractor or ride a horse? _____

Why? _____

. . . .

Farmer Fred has 12 chickens.
3 of them are roosters.
How many **hens** does Farmer Fred have?   9 hens

Farmer Fred collected 4 eggs on Monday,
5 eggs on Tuesday, and 3 eggs on Wednesday.
How many eggs did he collect altogether?   12 eggs

<small>© Evan-Moor Corp. • EMC 3391 • Critical and Creative Thinking Activities   75</small>

Page 76

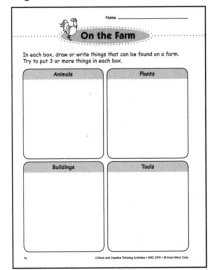

Name _____

On the Farm

In each box, draw or write things that can be found on a farm.
Try to put 3 or more things in each box.

Animals	Plants
Buildings	**Tools**

<small>76   Critical and Creative Thinking Activities • EMC 3391 • © Evan-Moor Corp.</small>

Page 77

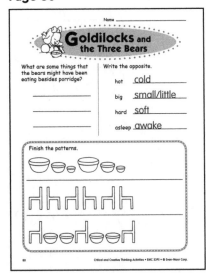

Name _____

In My Room

Put a O around things that are in your room.
Make an X on things that are <u>not</u> in your room.

bed	pizza	clock
bowling ball	toys	socks
books	pillow	desk
window	teddy bear	garden

What in your room begins with...

b? _____

s? _____

t? _____

p? _____

c? _____

Draw what you see from a window in your room or in your house.

<small>© Evan-Moor Corp. • EMC 3391 • Critical and Creative Thinking Activities   77</small>

Page 78

Name _____

In My Room

How is your room the **same** as the kitchen? _____

How is your room **different** from the kitchen? _____

Circle the 3 words that describe your room best.

cozy	big	noisy
dark	neat	small
cool	messy	cheerful

You are sitting on your bed. Which is closest? Circle it.

the door

the closet

the window

Name these things that can be found in a bedroom.

bed   dresser   door   window

<small>78   Critical and Creative Thinking Activities • EMC 3391 • © Evan-Moor Corp.</small>

Page 79

Name _____

In My Room

Derek is getting ready for school, but there are a lot of things wrong with his room.
Can you find at least 10? Circle them.
Then draw one more thing that is wrong.

<small>© Evan-Moor Corp. • EMC 3391 • Critical and Creative Thinking Activities   79</small>

Page 80

Name _____

Goldilocks and the Three Bears

What are some things that the bears might have been eating besides porridge?

_____
_____
_____

Write the opposite.

hot cold

big small/little

hard soft

asleep awake

Finish the patterns.

<small>80   Critical and Creative Thinking Activities • EMC 3391 • © Evan-Moor Corp.</small>

Page 81

Name _____

Goldilocks and the Three Bears

How are Goldilocks and Baby Bear the **same**? small/young/
hungry/both fit same chair, bed

How are they **different**?
Goldilocks is human. The bear is an animal.

. . . .

Do you think Goldilocks would make a good friend? _____

Why or why not? _____
_____
_____

How did Goldilocks feel when she...

wanted the porridge? hungry/starved

broke the chair? startled/scared/sorry

felt the beds? sleepy

saw the bears? frightened/scared

<small>© Evan-Moor Corp. • EMC 3391 • Critical and Creative Thinking Activities   81</small>

Page 82

Name _____

Goldilocks and the Three Bears

The second picture is different from the first picture in 8 ways.
Can you find them all? Circle them.
Then add two more things to the second picture.

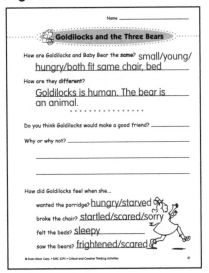

<small>82   Critical and Creative Thinking Activities • EMC 3391 • © Evan-Moor Corp.</small>

Page 83

The Three Billy Goats Gruff

Fill in the missing word.

The troll was <u>under</u> the bridge.

The goats went <u>over</u> the bridge.

The troll was pushed <u>down</u> the river.

Write the opposite.

big <u>little</u>   mean <u>nice</u>

ugly <u>pretty/beautiful</u>   under <u>over</u>

Color big goats blue.
Color medium goats yellow.
Color small goats green.

Page 84

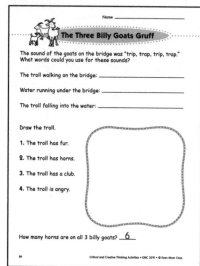

The Three Billy Goats Gruff

The sound of the goats on the bridge was "trip, trap, trip, trap."
What words could you use for these sounds?

The troll walking on the bridge: _____

Water running under the bridge: _____

The troll falling into the water: _____

Draw the troll.

1. The troll has fur.

2. The troll has horns.

3. The troll has a club.

4. The troll is angry.

How many horns are on all 3 billy goats? <u>6</u>

Page 85

The Three Billy Goats Gruff

Describe each picture with 2 rhyming words.

<u>goat</u> in a <u>boat</u>   <u>troll</u> in a <u>hole</u>

<u>bear</u> on a <u>chair</u>   <u>pig</u> in a <u>wig</u>

<u>bread</u> in <u>bed</u>   <u>whale</u> in <u>jail</u>

Page 86

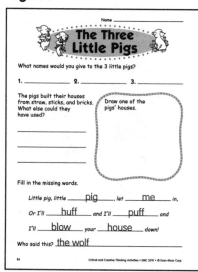

The Three Little Pigs

What names would you give to the 3 little pigs?

1. _____ 2. _____ 3. _____

The pigs built their houses from straw, sticks, and bricks. What else could they have used?

Draw one of the pigs' houses.

_____

_____

_____

Fill in the missing words.

Little pig, little <u>pig</u>, let <u>me</u> in,

Or I'll <u>huff</u> and I'll <u>puff</u> and

I'll <u>blow</u> your <u>house</u> down!

Who said this? <u>the wolf</u>

Page 87

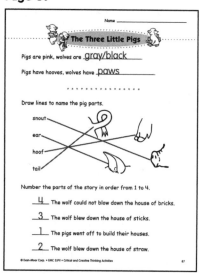

The Three Little Pigs

Pigs are pink, wolves are <u>gray/black</u>

Pigs have hooves, wolves have <u>paws</u>

Draw lines to name the pig parts.

snout
ear
hoof
tail

Number the parts of the story in order from 1 to 4.

<u>4</u> The wolf could not blow down the house of bricks.

<u>3</u> The wolf blew down the house of sticks.

<u>1</u> The pigs went off to build their houses.

<u>2</u> The wolf blew down the house of straw.

Page 88

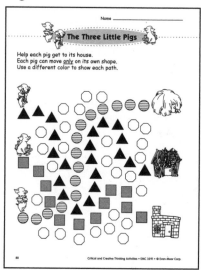

The Three Little Pigs

Help each pig get to its house.
Each pig can move only on its own shape.
Use a different color to show each path.

Page 89

The Gingerbread Man

Fill in the missing words.

Run, <u>run</u> as <u>fast</u> as <u>you</u> can.

You <u>can't</u> catch <u>me</u>, I'm

<u>the</u> Gingerbread <u>Man</u>!

Why did the Gingerbread Man run away?

_____

These are tasty gingerbread men.

These are not tasty gingerbread men.

Draw a tasty gingerbread man.

Drawings should have 3 buttons.

Page 90

The Gingerbread Man

Which one does not belong?

SUGAR

Would you eat a talking gingerbread man? _____

Why or why not? _____

Circle the gingerbread man that is different.

Page 91

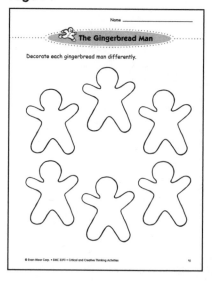

The Gingerbread Man

Decorate each gingerbread man differently.

Critical and Creative Thinking Activities • EMC 3391 • © Evan-Moor Corp.

Page 92

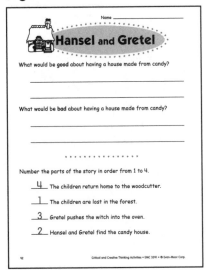

Hansel and Gretel

What would be **good** about having a house made from candy?

_____

_____

What would be **bad** about having a house made from candy?

_____

_____

• • • • • • • • • • • • • •

Number the parts of the story in order from 1 to 4.

__4__ The children return home to the woodcutter.

__1__ The children are lost in the forest.

__3__ Gretel pushes the witch into the oven.

__2__ Hansel and Gretel find the candy house.

Page 93

Hansel and Gretel

If the witch's house had been made from vegetables instead of candy, would the children still have come inside?

_____

Why or why not?

_____

_____

Draw a vegetable house.

• • • • • • • • • • • • • •

What kinds of candies would be best for making a…

fence? _____

door? _____

roof? _____

chimney? _____

Page 94

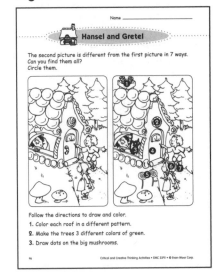

Hansel and Gretel

The second picture is different from the first picture in 7 ways. Can you find them all? Circle them.

Follow the directions to draw and color.

1. Color each roof in a different pattern.

2. Make the trees 3 different colors of green.

3. Draw dots on the big mushrooms.

Page 95

Cars, Trucks, and Buses

Do you think it would be fun to drive a big cargo truck?

Why or why not? _____

What is wrong with this picture?

Match each with what it carries.

The truck should be bigger than the car.

How long was your **longest** car trip? _____

Where did you go? _____

Page 96

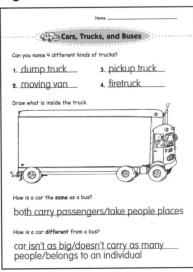

Cars, Trucks, and Buses

Can you name 4 different kinds of trucks?

1. dump truck   3. pickup truck

2. moving van   4. firetruck

Draw what is inside the truck.

How is a car the **same** as a bus?

both carry passengers/take people places

How is a car **different** from a bus?

car isn't as big/doesn't carry as many people/belongs to an individual

Page 97

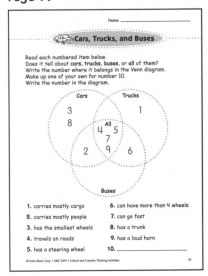

Cars, Trucks, and Buses

Read each numbered item below.
Does it tell about **cars**, **trucks**, **buses**, or all of them?
Write the number where it belongs in the Venn diagram.
Make up one of your own for number 10.
Write the number in the diagram.

Cars   Trucks

3   1

8   All 5

4
7

2   9   6

Buses

1. carries mostly cargo   6. can have more than 4 wheels

2. carries mostly people   7. can go fast

3. has the smallest wheels   8. has a trunk

4. travels on roads   9. has a loud horn

5. has a steering wheel   10. _____

Page 98

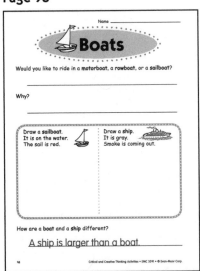

Boats

Would you like to ride in a **motorboat**, a **rowboat**, or a **sailboat**?

_____

Why?

_____

Draw a **sailboat**.
It is on the water.
The sail is red.

Draw a **ship**.
It is gray.
Smoke is coming out.

How are a **boat** and a **ship** different?

A ship is larger than a boat.

Page 99

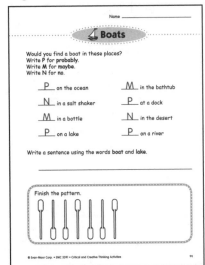

Boats

Would you find a boat in these places?
Write P for **probably**.
Write M for **maybe**.
Write N for **no**.

__P__ on the ocean   __M__ in the bathtub

__N__ in a salt shaker   __P__ at a dock

__M__ in a bottle   __N__ in the desert

__P__ on a lake   __P__ on a river

Write a sentence using the words **boat** and **lake**.

_____

Finish the pattern.

Page 100

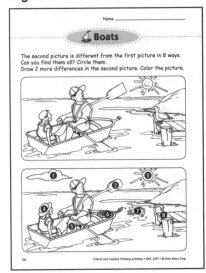

Boats

The second picture is different from the first picture in 8 ways. Can you find them all? Circle them.
Draw 2 more differences in the second picture. Color the picture.

Page 101

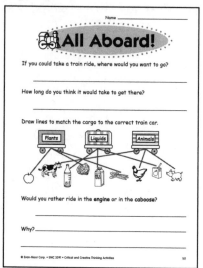

All Aboard!

If you could take a train ride, where would you want to go?

How long do you think it would take to get there?

Draw lines to match the cargo to the correct train car.

Plants   Liquids   Animals

Would you rather ride in the **engine** or in the **caboose**?

Why?

Page 102

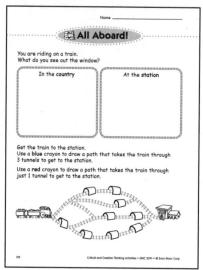

All Aboard!

You are riding on a train.
What do you see out the window?

| In the country | At the station |

Get the train to the station.
Use a **blue** crayon to draw a path that takes the train through 3 tunnels to get to the station.

Use a **red** crayon to draw a path that takes the train through just 1 tunnel to get to the station.

Page 103

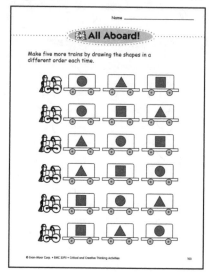

All Aboard!

Make five more trains by drawing the shapes in a different order each time.

Page 104

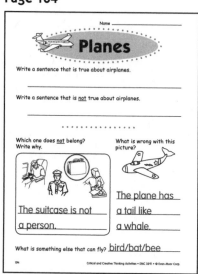

Planes

Write a sentence that is true about airplanes.

Write a sentence that is **not** true about airplanes.

Which one does **not** belong? Write why.

The suitcase is not a person.

What is wrong with this picture?

The plane has a tail like a whale.

What is something else that can fly? bird/bat/bee

Page 105

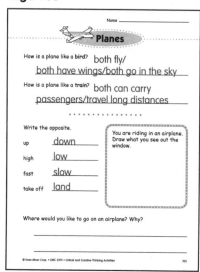

Planes

How is a plane like a **bird**? both fly/
both have wings/both go in the sky

How is a plane like a **train**? both can carry
passengers/travel long distances

Write the opposite.

up   down
high   low
fast   slow
take off   land

You are riding in an airplane. Draw what you see out the window.

Where would you like to go on an airplane? Why?

Page 106

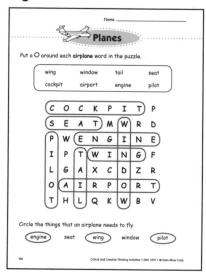

Planes

Put a O around each **airplane** word in the puzzle.

| wing | window | tail | seat |
| cockpit | airport | engine | pilot |

```
C O C K P I T P
S E A T M W R D
P W E N G I N E
I P T W I N G F
L G A X C D Z R
O A I R P O R T
T H L Q K W B V
```

Circle the things that an airplane needs to fly.

engine   seat   wing   window   pilot

Page 107

Bikes

A car has 4 wheels. A bike has 2 wheels.

A car has a steering wheel. A bike has handlebars

In a car, you wear a seat belt.

On a bike, you wear a helmet

Which picture is different? Circle it.

Circle the things that you have done on a bike.
Cross off the things that you have **not** done on a bike.

gone down a hill   wiped out

done a "wheelie"   rode on a bike trail

rode through a puddle   rode double

Page 108

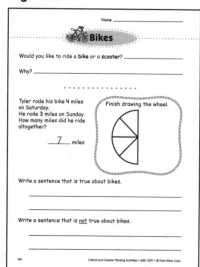

Bikes

Would you like to ride a **bike** or a **scooter**?

Why?

Tyler rode his bike 4 miles on Saturday.
He rode 3 miles on Sunday.
How many miles did he ride altogether?

7 miles

Finish drawing the wheel.

Write a sentence that is true about bikes.

Write a sentence that is **not** true about bikes.

Page 109

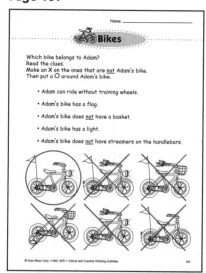

Bikes

Which bike belongs to Adam?
Read the clues.
Make an X on the ones that are **not** Adam's bike.
Then put a O around Adam's bike.

• Adam can ride without training wheels.

• Adam's bike has a flag.

• Adam's bike does **not** have a basket.

• Adam's bike has a light.

• Adam's bike does **not** have streamers on the handlebars.

Page 110

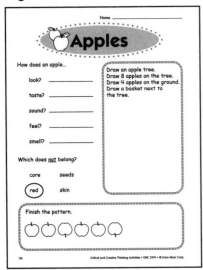

Apples

How does an apple…

look? _____

taste? _____

sound? _____

feel? _____

smell? _____

Draw an apple tree.
Draw 8 apples on the tree.
Draw 4 apples on the ground.
Draw a basket next to the tree.

Which does _not_ belong?

core   seeds

(red)   skin

Finish the pattern.

Page 111

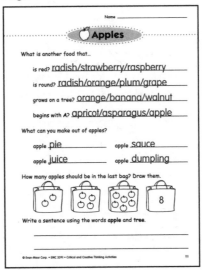

Apples

What is another food that…

is red? radish/strawberry/raspberry

is round? radish/orange/plum/grape

grows on a tree? orange/banana/walnut

begins with A? apricot/asparagus/apple

What can you make out of apples?

apple pie   apple sauce

apple juice   apple dumpling

How many apples should be in the last bag? Draw them.

8

Write a sentence using the words **apple** and **tree**.

_____

Page 112

Apples

Morgan and her mom are making an apple pie.
Number the pictures from 1 to 6 to show the correct order.

4   3   6

1   2   5

On the back, write or draw what _you_ would like to put in a pie.

Page 113

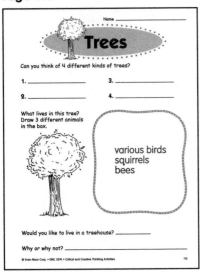

Trees

Can you think of 4 different kinds of trees?

1. _____   3. _____

2. _____   4. _____

What lives in this tree?
Draw 3 different animals in the box.

various birds
squirrels
bees

Would you like to live in a treehouse? _____

Why or why not? _____

Page 114

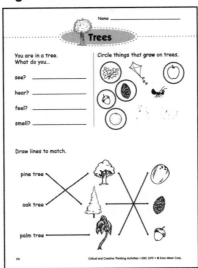

Trees

You are in a tree. What do you…

see? _____

hear? _____

feel? _____

smell? _____

Circle things that grow on trees.

Draw lines to match.

pine tree

oak tree

palm tree

Page 115

Trees

Help the squirrel get to its stash of nuts.
Be sure not to run into any other animals!

Page 116

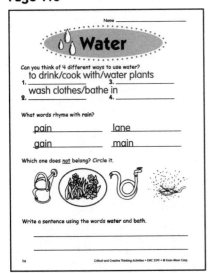

Water

Can you think of 4 different ways to use water?

1. to drink/cook with/water plants

2. wash clothes/bathe in

3.

4.

What words rhyme with rain?

pain   lane

gain   main

Which one does _not_ belong? Circle it.

Write a sentence using the words **water** and **bath**.

_____

Page 117

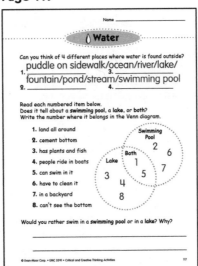

Water

Can you think of 4 different places where water is found outside?

1. puddle on sidewalk/ocean/river/lake/

2. fountain/pond/stream/swimming pool

3.

4.

Read each numbered item below.
Does it tell about a **swimming pool**, a **lake**, or **both**?
Write the number where it belongs in the Venn diagram.

1. land all around
2. cement bottom
3. has plants and fish
4. people ride in boats
5. can swim in it
6. have to clean it
7. in a backyard
8. can't see the bottom

Swimming Pool
2   6
Both
7
Lake
1   5
4
8
3

Would you rather swim in a **swimming pool** or in a lake? Why?

_____

Page 118

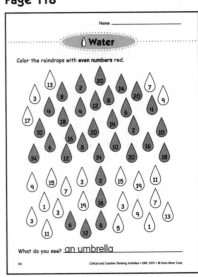

Water

Color the raindrops with **even numbers** red.

What do you see? an umbrella

Page 119

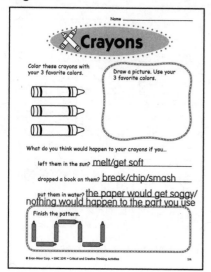

Crayons

Color these crayons with your 3 favorite colors.

Draw a picture. Use your 3 favorite colors.

What do you think would happen to your crayons if you...

left them in the sun? melt/get soft

dropped a book on them? break/chip/smash

put them in water? the paper would get soggy/ nothing would happen to the part you use

Finish the pattern.

Page 120

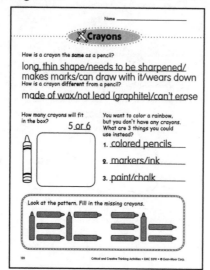

Crayons

How is a crayon **same** as a pencil?

long, thin shape/needs to be sharpened/ makes marks/can draw with it/wears down

How is a crayon **different** from a pencil?

made of wax/not lead (graphite)/can't erase

How many crayons will fit in the box?   5 or 6

You want to color a rainbow, but you don't have any crayons. What are 3 things you could use instead?

1. colored pencils

2. markers/ink

3. paint/chalk

Look at the pattern. Fill in the missing crayons.

Page 121

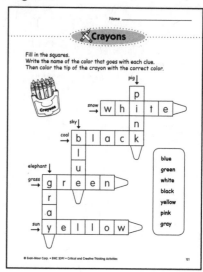

Crayons

Fill in the squares.
Write the name of the color that goes with each clue.
Then color the tip of the crayon with the correct color.

snow → w h i t e

pig → p

sky → l

coal → b l a c k

elephant → u

grass → g r e e n

r

a

sun → y e l l o w

blue
green
white
black
yellow
pink
gray

Page 122

Vegetables

There are so many kinds of vegetables!
Draw a line under the ones that you have tried.
Circle the ones that you like.

corn   carrots   zucchini   cucumber

celery   broccoli   asparagus   cauliflower

peas   lettuce   potatoes   green beans

Which one does **not** belong?

Draw your favorite vegetable.

Page 123

Vegetables

Which do you like?
Number the vegetables from 1 to 6.
The one you like the most should be number 1.

____ peas

____ spinach

____ carrots

____ corn

____ green beans

____ celery

What is a vegetable that you do **not** like?

_____

Draw a head using only vegetables.

What vegetables did you use?

eyes: _____

nose: _____

mouth: _____

ears: _____

hair: _____

Page 124

Vegetables

Read the clues to find the mystery vegetables!

I am orange.
Rabbits like me.
I grow underground.

I am a carrot

I am green.
I am in most salads.
You eat my leaves.

I am lettuce

I am green.
I am used to make pickles.
I start with C.

I am a cucumber

We are green.
We are small and round.
We grow in a pod.

We are peas

I am yellow.
I grow on a stalk.
You can eat me off the cob.

I am corn

I am brown on the outside.
I am white on the inside.
I grow underground.

I am a potato

Page 125

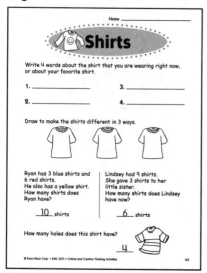

Shirts

Write 4 words about the shirt that you are wearing right now, or about your favorite shirt.

1. _____   3. _____

2. _____   4. _____

Draw to make the shirts different in 3 ways.

Ryan has 3 blue shirts and 6 red shirts.
He also has a yellow shirt.
How many shirts does Ryan have?

10 shirts

Lindsey had 9 shirts.
She gave 3 shirts to her little sister.
How many shirts does Lindsey have now?

6 shirts

How many holes does this shirt have?

4

Page 126

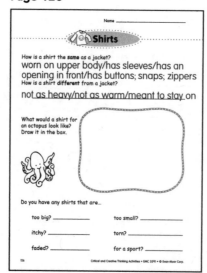

Shirts

How is a shirt **same** as a jacket?

worn on upper body/has sleeves/has an opening in front/has buttons; snaps; zippers

How is a shirt **different** from a jacket?

not as heavy/not as warm/meant to stay on

What would a shirt for an octopus look like?
Draw it in the box.

Do you have any shirts that are...

too big? _____   too small? _____

itchy? _____   torn? _____

faded? _____   for a sport? _____

Page 127

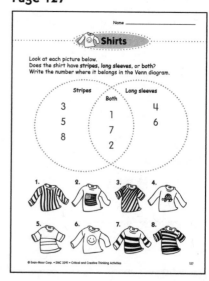

Shirts

Look at each picture below.
Does the shirt have **stripes, long sleeves,** or **both**?
Write the number where it belongs in the Venn diagram.

Stripes   Long sleeves

Both

3
5
8

1
7
2

4
6

1.   2.   3.   4.

5.   6.   7.   8.

Page 128

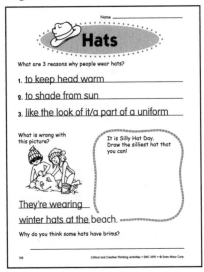

Hats

What are 3 reasons why people wear hats?

1. to keep head warm
2. to shade from sun
3. like the look of it/a part of a uniform

What is wrong with this picture?

It is Silly Hat Day. Draw the silliest hat that you can!

They're wearing winter hats at the beach.

Why do you think some hats have brims?

Page 129

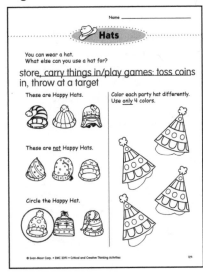

Hats

You can wear a hat. What else can you use a hat for?

store, carry things in/play games: toss coins in, throw at a target

These are Happy Hats.

These are not Happy Hats.

Circle the Happy Hat.

Color each party hat differently. Use only 4 colors.

Page 130

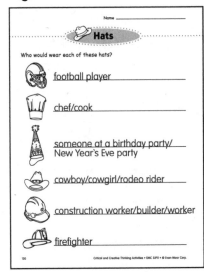

Hats

Who would wear each of these hats?

football player

chef/cook

someone at a birthday party/ New Year's Eve party

cowboy/cowgirl/rodeo rider

construction worker/builder/worker

firefighter

Page 131

Ice Cream

What is your favorite flavor of ice cream? _____

Do you like it in a cone or in a dish? _____

You are making an ice-cream sundae. Circle the things that you will use.

Draw your sundae.

Write a sentence using the words ice cream and melt.

Page 132

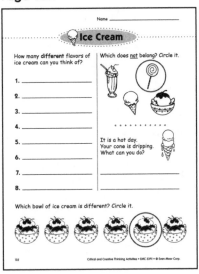

Ice Cream

How many different flavors of ice cream can you think of?

1. _____
2. _____
3. _____
4. _____
5. _____
6. _____
7. _____
8. _____

Which does not belong? Circle it.

It is a hot day. Your cone is dripping. What can you do?

Which bowl of ice cream is different? Circle it.

Page 133

Ice Cream

Which ice-cream treat did Anna eat? Read the clues. Make an X on the ones that are not Anna's treat. Then put a O around Anna's treat.

• Anna got only one scoop of ice cream.

• Anna does not like cherries.

• Anna's ice cream is not in a dish.

• Anna got sprinkles on her ice cream.

Page 134

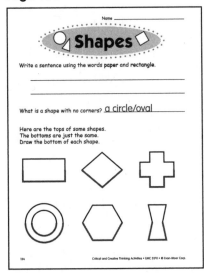

Shapes

Write a sentence using the words paper and rectangle.

What is a shape with no corners? a circle/oval

Here are the tops of some shapes. The bottoms are just the same. Draw the bottom of each shape.

Page 135

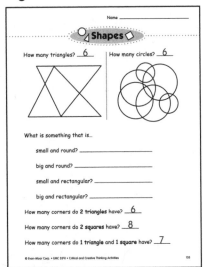

Shapes

How many triangles? 6   How many circles? 6

What is something that is...

small and round? _____

big and round? _____

small and rectangular? _____

big and rectangular? _____

How many corners do 2 triangles have? 6

How many corners do 2 squares have? 8

How many corners do 1 triangle and 1 square have? 7

Page 136

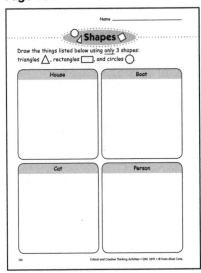

Shapes

Draw the things listed below using only 3 shapes: triangles △, rectangles ▭, and circles ○.

House	Boat
Cat	Person

Page 137

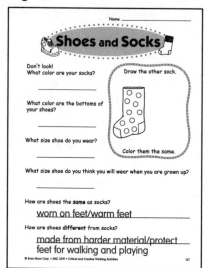

Shoes and Socks

Don't look!
What color are your socks?
_____

What color are the bottoms of
your shoes?
_____

What size shoe do you wear?
_____

Draw the other sock.

Color them the same.

What size shoe do you think you will wear when you are grown up?
_____

How are shoes the **same** as socks?
worn on feet/warm feet

How are shoes **different** from socks?
made from harder material/protect
feet for walking and playing

© Evan-Moor Corp. • EMC 3391 • Critical and Creative Thinking Activities   137

Page 138

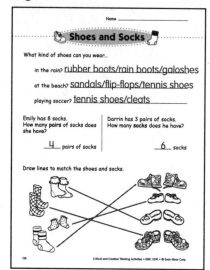

Shoes and Socks

What kind of shoes can you wear...

in the rain? rubber boots/rain boots/galoshes

at the beach? sandals/flip-flops/tennis shoes

playing soccer? tennis shoes/cleats

Emily has 8 socks.
How many **pairs** of socks does
she have?

___4___ pairs of socks

Darrin has 3 pairs of socks.
How many **socks** does he have?

___6___ socks

Draw lines to match the shoes and socks.

138   Critical and Creative Thinking Activities • EMC 3391 • © Evan-Moor Corp.

Page 139

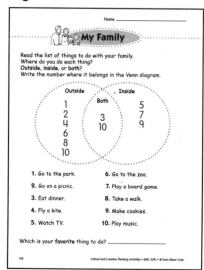

Shoes and Socks

Find the matching shoes.
Color them the same.

© Evan-Moor Corp. • EMC 3391 • Critical and Creative Thinking Activities   139

Page 140

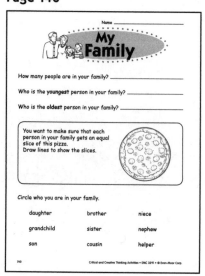

My Family

How many people are in your family? _____

Who is the **youngest** person in your family? _____

Who is the **oldest** person in your family? _____

You want to make sure that each
person in your family gets an equal
slice of this pizza.
Draw lines to show the slices.

Circle who you are in your family.

daughter	brother	niece
grandchild	sister	nephew
son	cousin	helper

140   Critical and Creative Thinking Activities • EMC 3391 • © Evan-Moor Corp.

Page 141

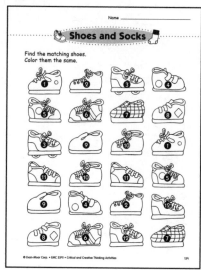

My Family

Your mother's mother is your grandmother

Your father's sister is your aunt

What do you think is the hardest thing about being a **child**?
_____
_____

What do you think is the hardest thing about being a **parent**?
_____
_____

Draw 3 things that are important to your family.

© Evan-Moor Corp. • EMC 3391 • Critical and Creative Thinking Activities   141

Page 142

My Family

Read the list of things to do with your family.
Where do you do each thing?
Outside, inside, or both?
Write the number where it belongs in the Venn diagram.

Outside   Inside
        Both

1   5
2   3   7
4   10   9
6
8
10

1. Go to the park.
2. Go on a picnic.
3. Eat dinner.
4. Fly a kite.
5. Watch TV.

6. Go to the zoo.
7. Play a board game.
8. Take a walk.
9. Make cookies.
10. Play music.

Which is your **favorite** thing to do? _____

142   Critical and Creative Thinking Activities • EMC 3391 • © Evan-Moor Corp.

Evan-Moor's
Daily Plan & Daily Record Books

Two must-have teacher resources with three fun themes to choose from!

Daily Plan Books

Organize your entire school year—and with style! Original artwork brings a touch of fun to these spiral-bound planners. 96 pages.

Daily Plan Book: School Days
All Grades   EMC 5400

Daily Plan Book: Garden Days
All Grades   EMC 5401

Daily Plan Book: Animal Academy
All Grades   EMC 5402

Animal Academy

School Days

Garden Days

Daily Record Books

Finally, all the forms you need to track and record student progress in one spot! 96 pages.

Daily Record Book: School Days
All Grades   EMC 5403

Daily Record Book: Garden Days
All Grades   EMC 5404

Daily Record Book: Animal Academy
All Grades   EMC 5405

Must-have resources that make learning fun!

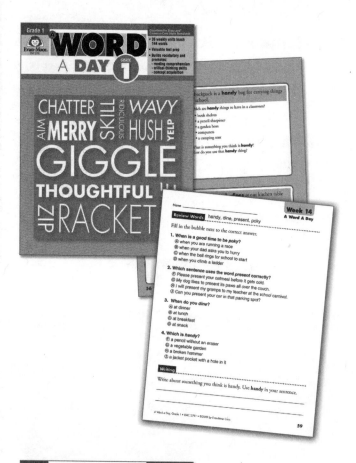

A Word a Day

Help your students develop the rich and diverse vocabulary they need for academic success!

Research shows that strong vocabulary and word knowledge is directly linked to academic accomplishment. Make sure your students develop the rich vocabulary that's essential to successful reading comprehension and academic achievement with *A Word a Day*. Each book in this newly revised series covers 144 words in 36 engaging weekly units. And with new features, such as an oral review and a written assessment for each week, it's easier than ever to help your students develop the vocabulary they need.

Grade 1	EMC 2791
Grade 2	EMC 2792
Grade 3	EMC 2793
Grade 4	EMC 2794
Grade 5	EMC 2795
Grade 6	EMC 2796

Thinking Skills

Help your students practice thinking skills with the creative and engaging activities in the *Thinking Skills* series. The 44 imaginative lessons in each book include downloadable interactive charts and reproducible practice pages to help your students think creatively, logically, and critically.

Grades 1–2	EMC 5301
Grades 3–4	EMC 5302
Grades 5–6	EMC 5303